ORGANICA

ARTWORK BY:
KEVIN HARDEN

KEVINHARDEN.NET

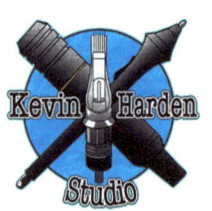 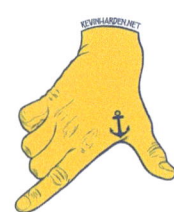 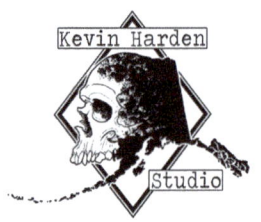

ORGANICA IS COPYRIGHT © 2018 KEVIN HARDEN

ALL ARTWORK COPYRIGHT © 2018 KEVIN HARDEN

No portion of this book can be reproduced without notarized written permission from Kevin Harden

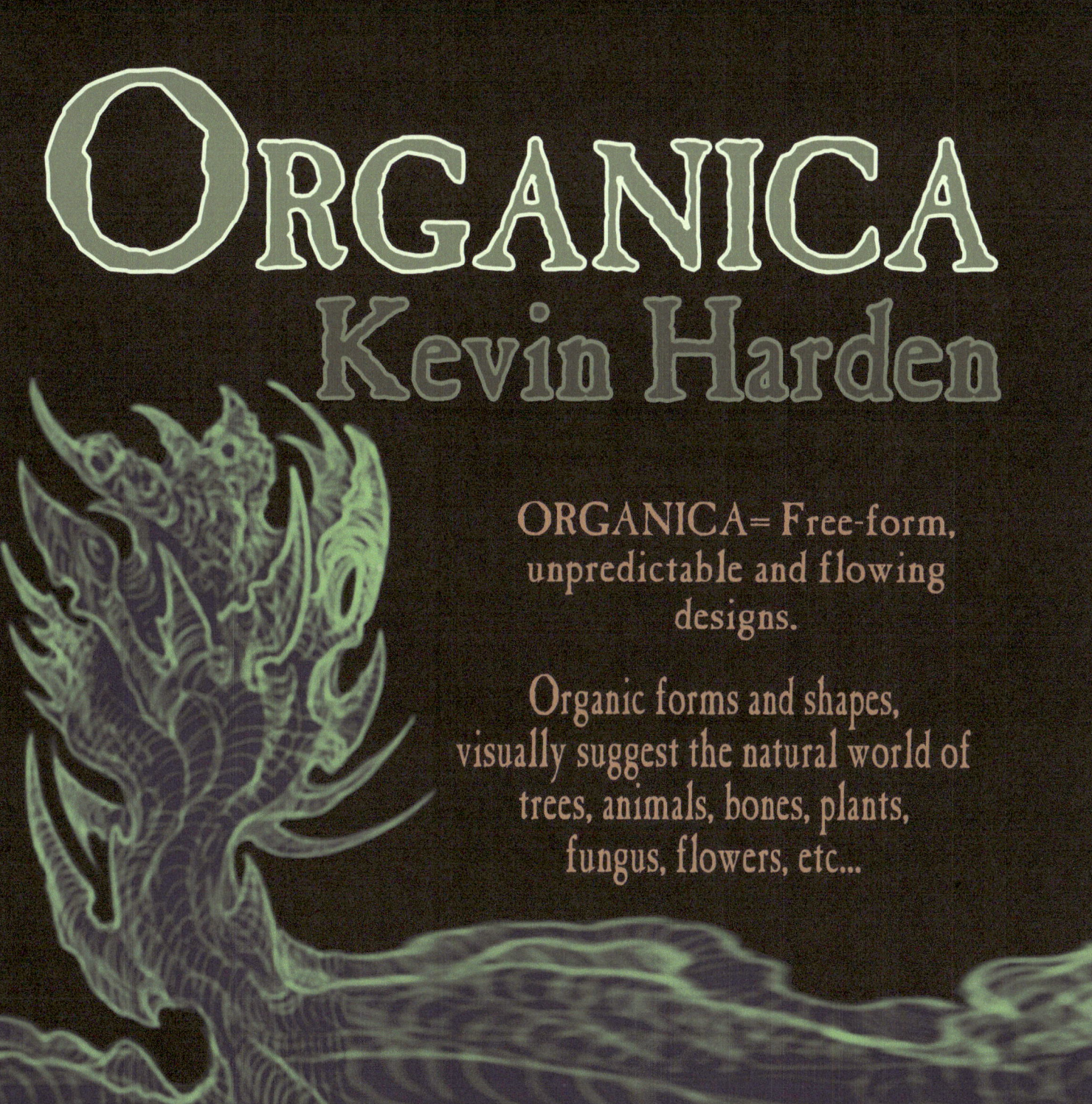

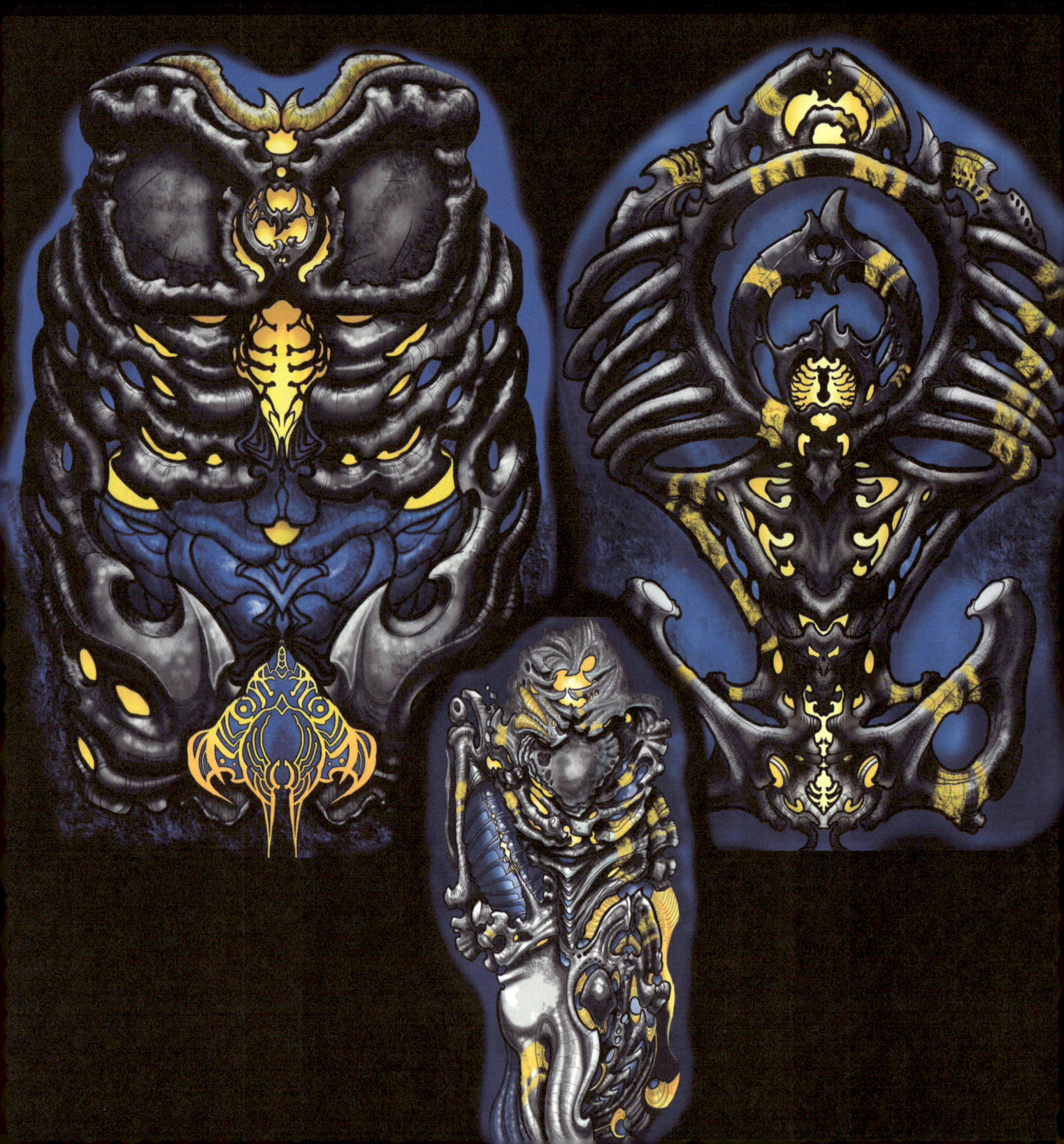

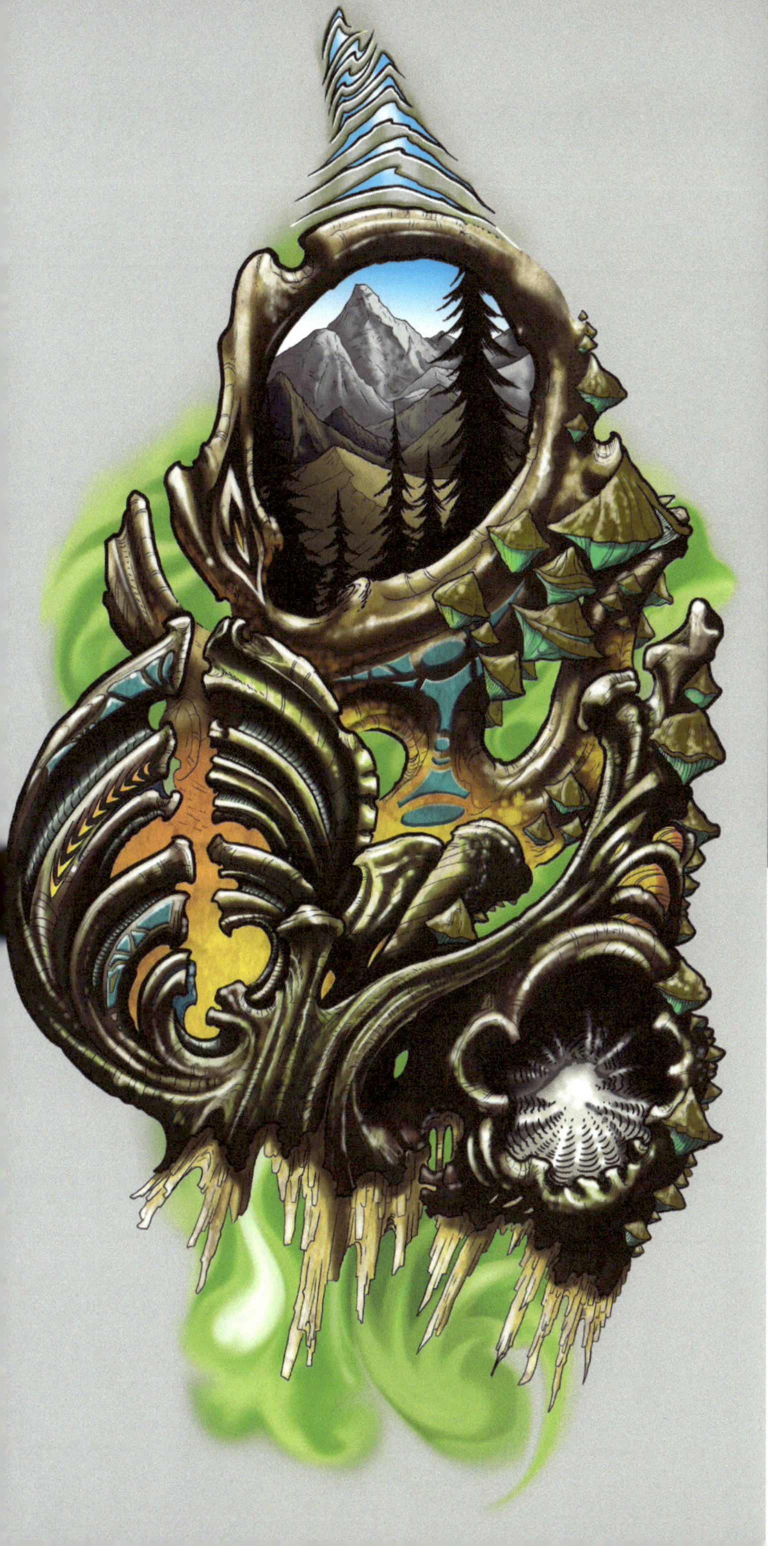

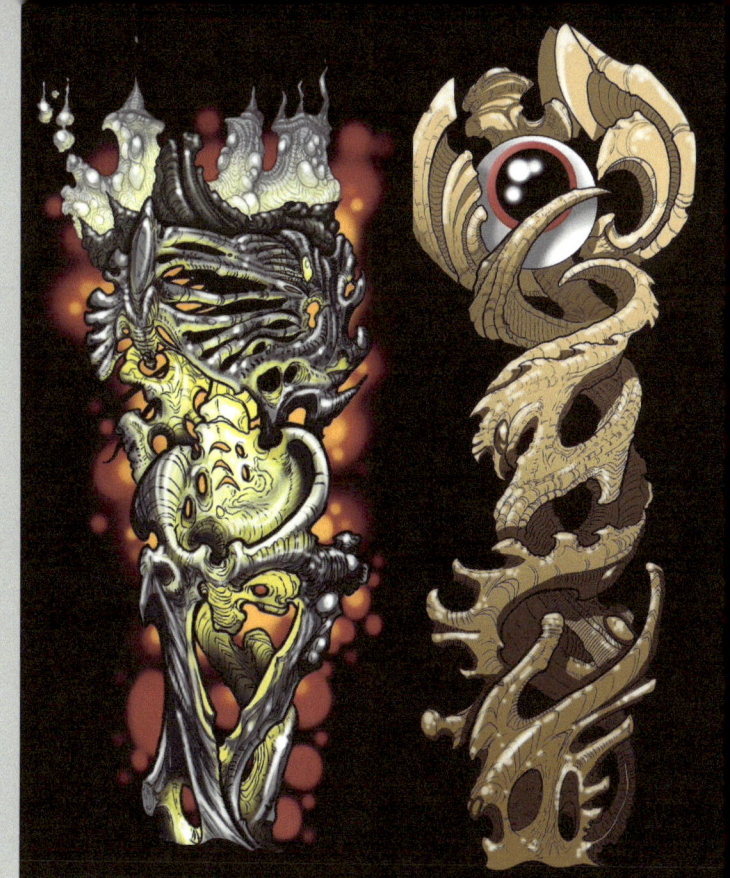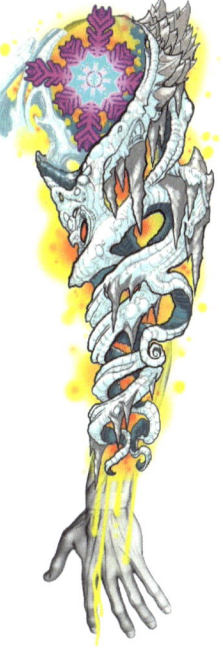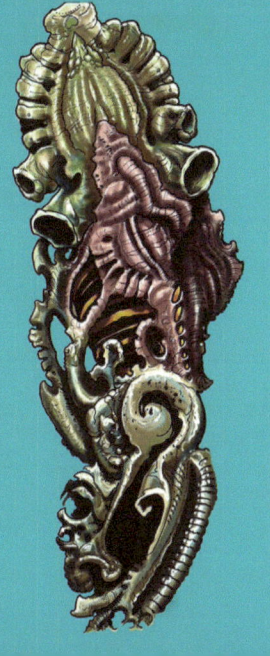

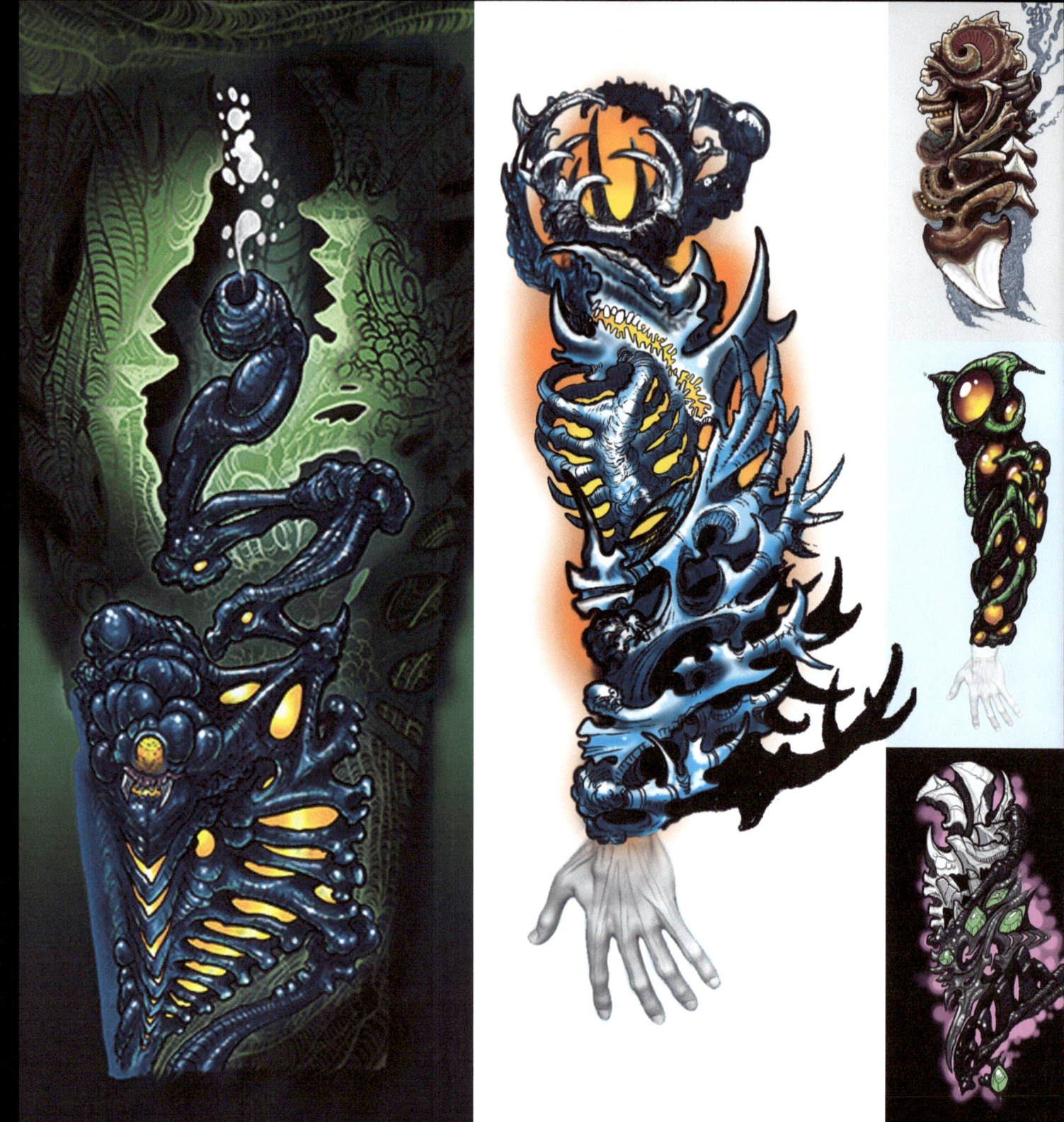

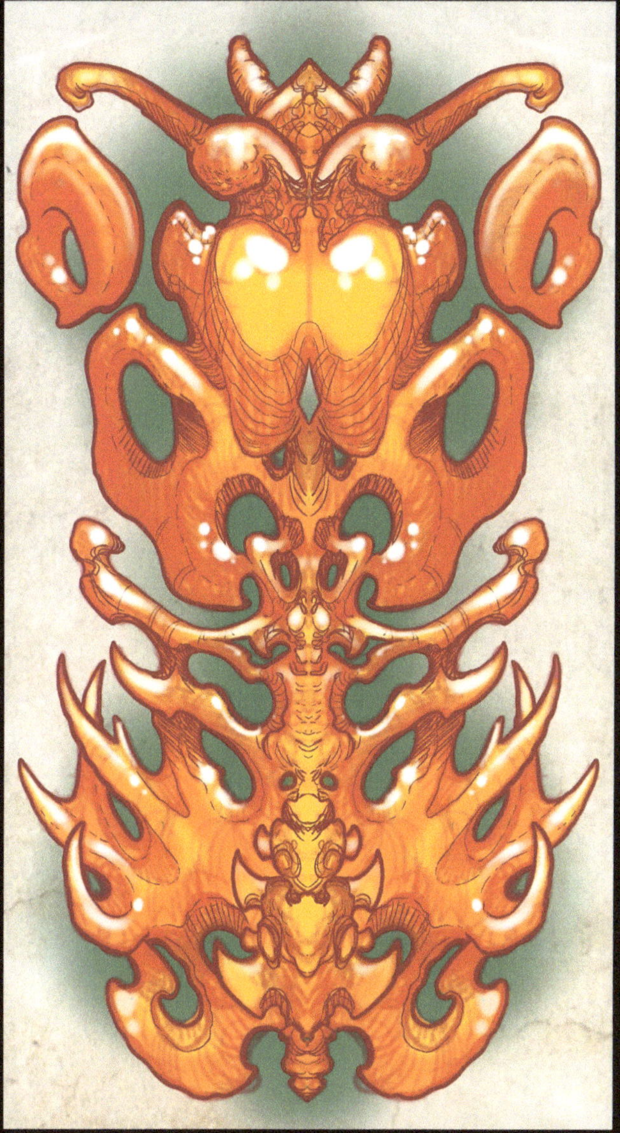

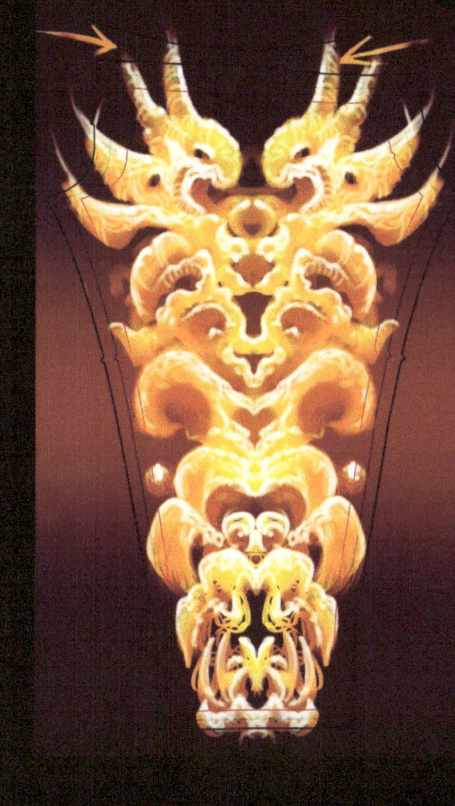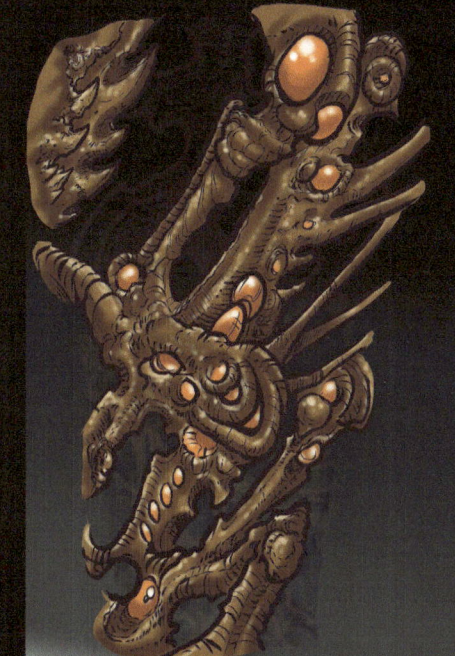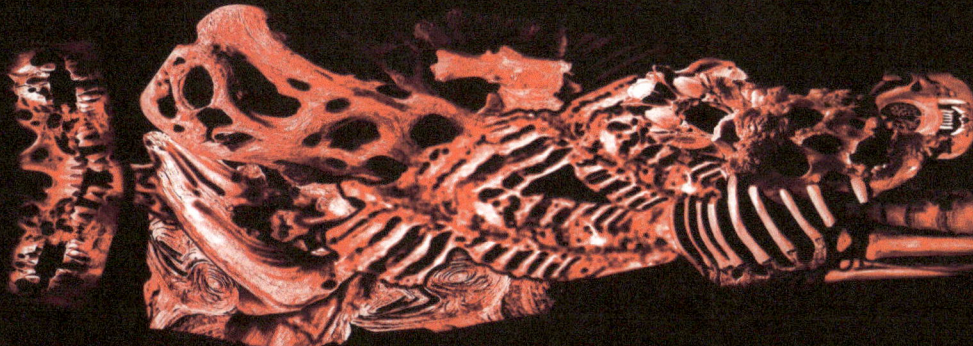

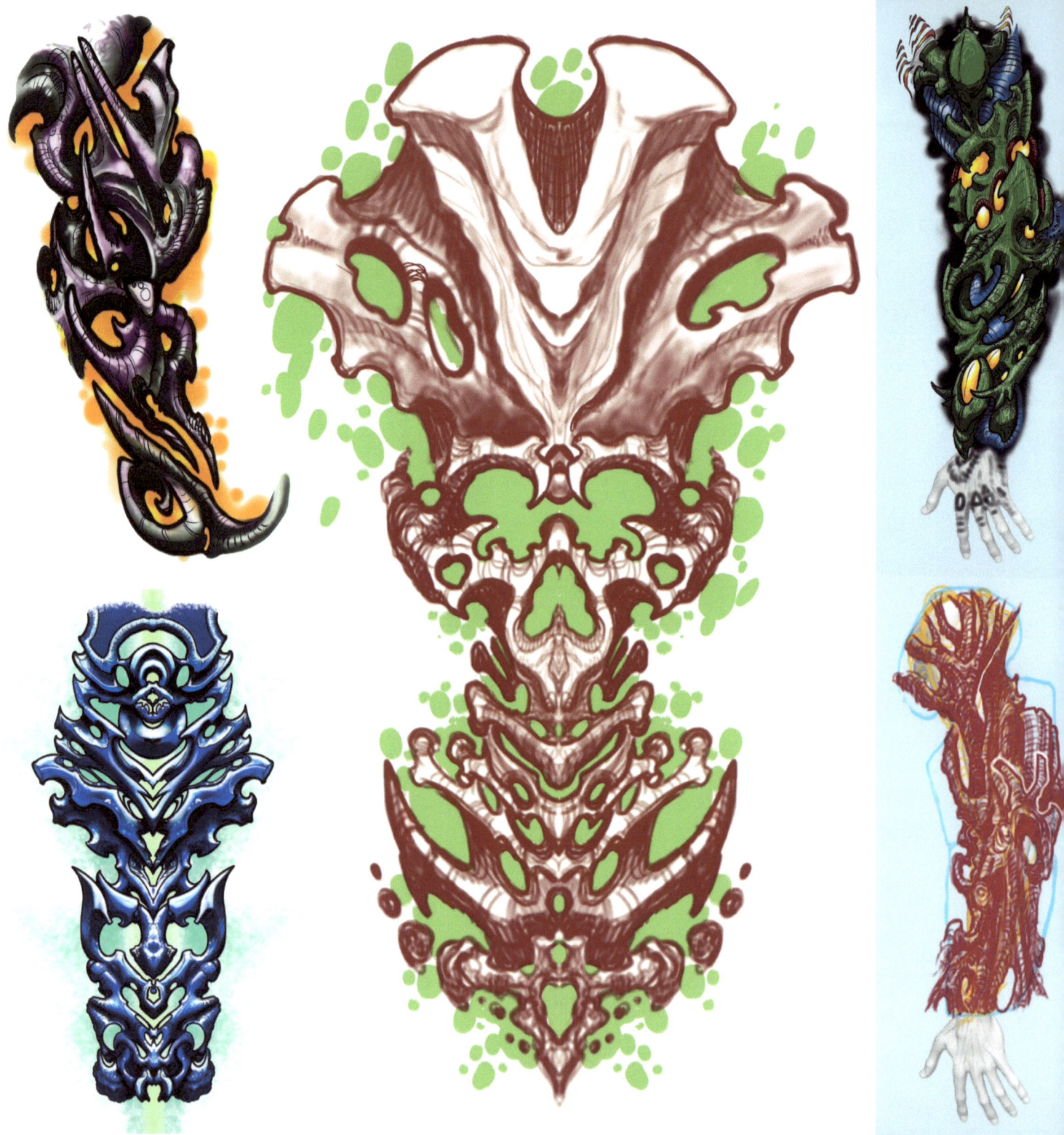

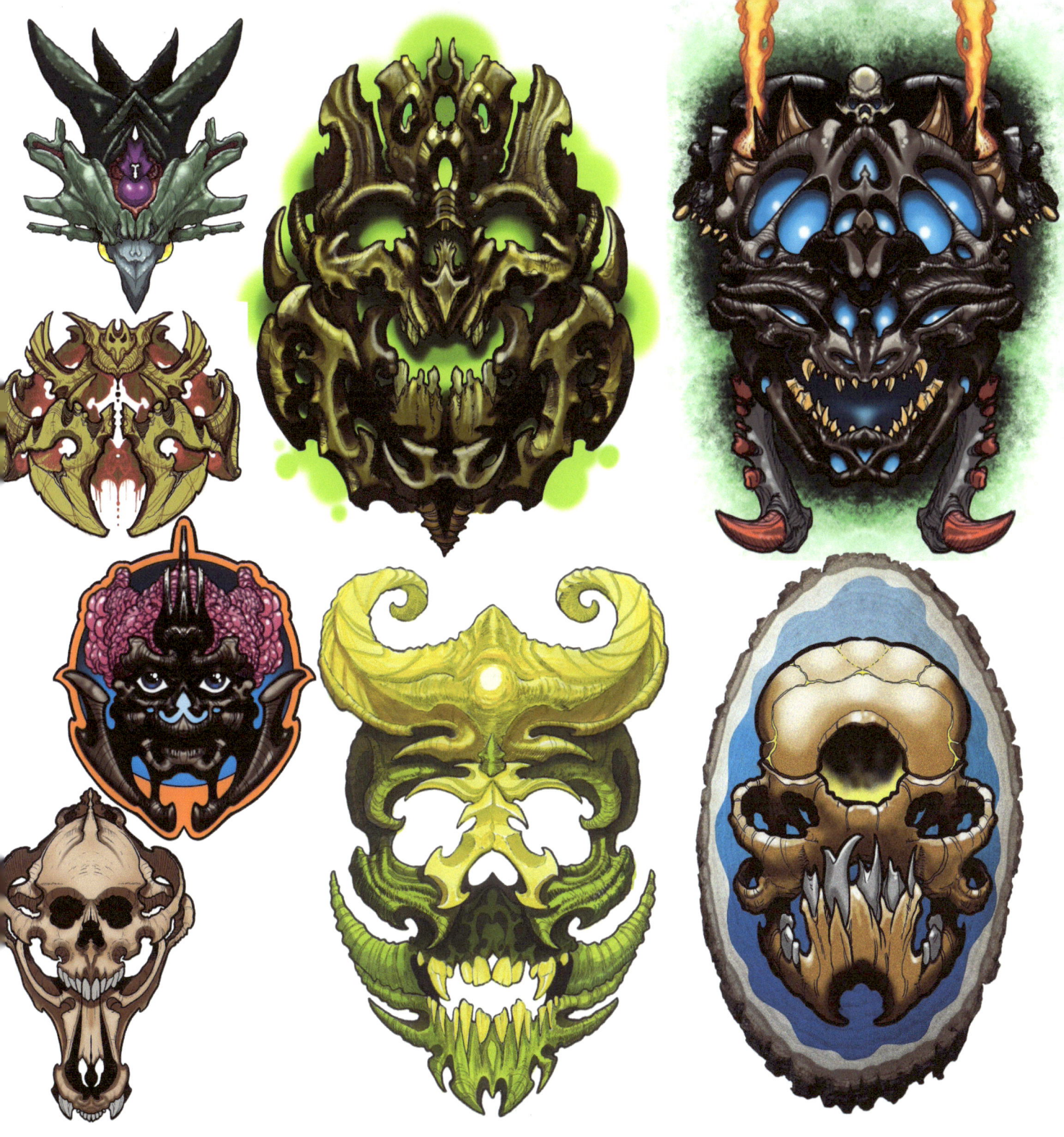

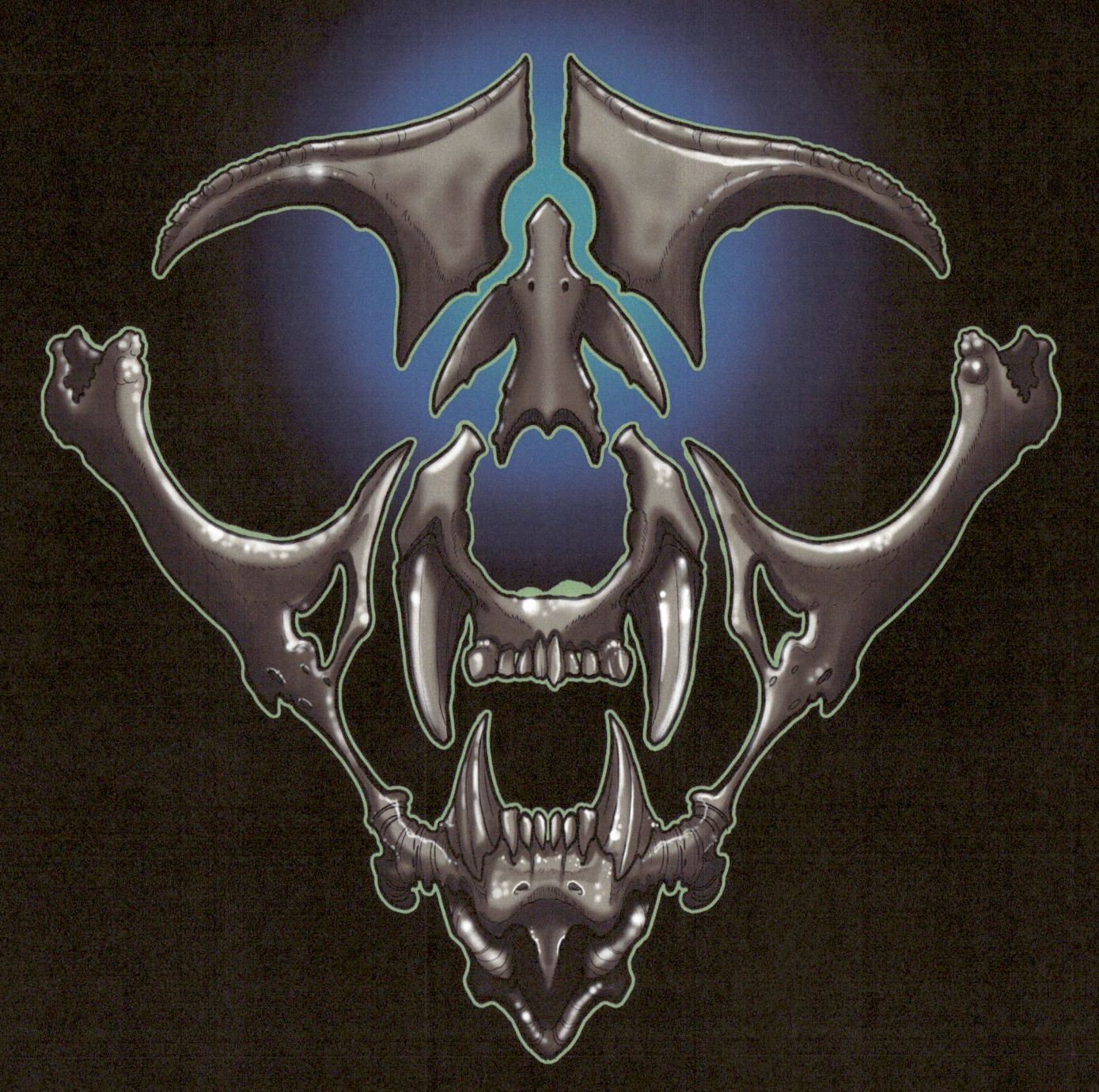

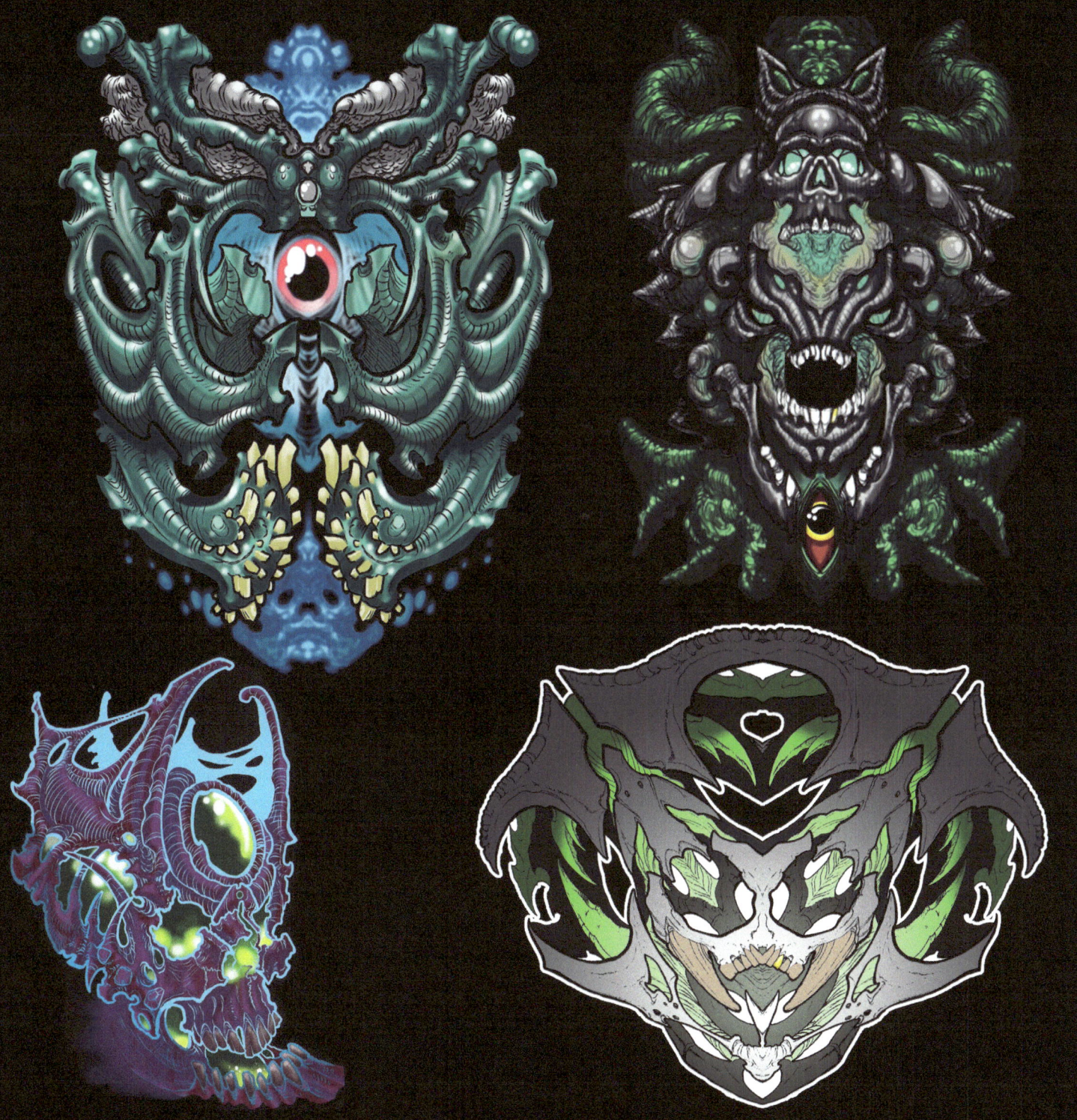

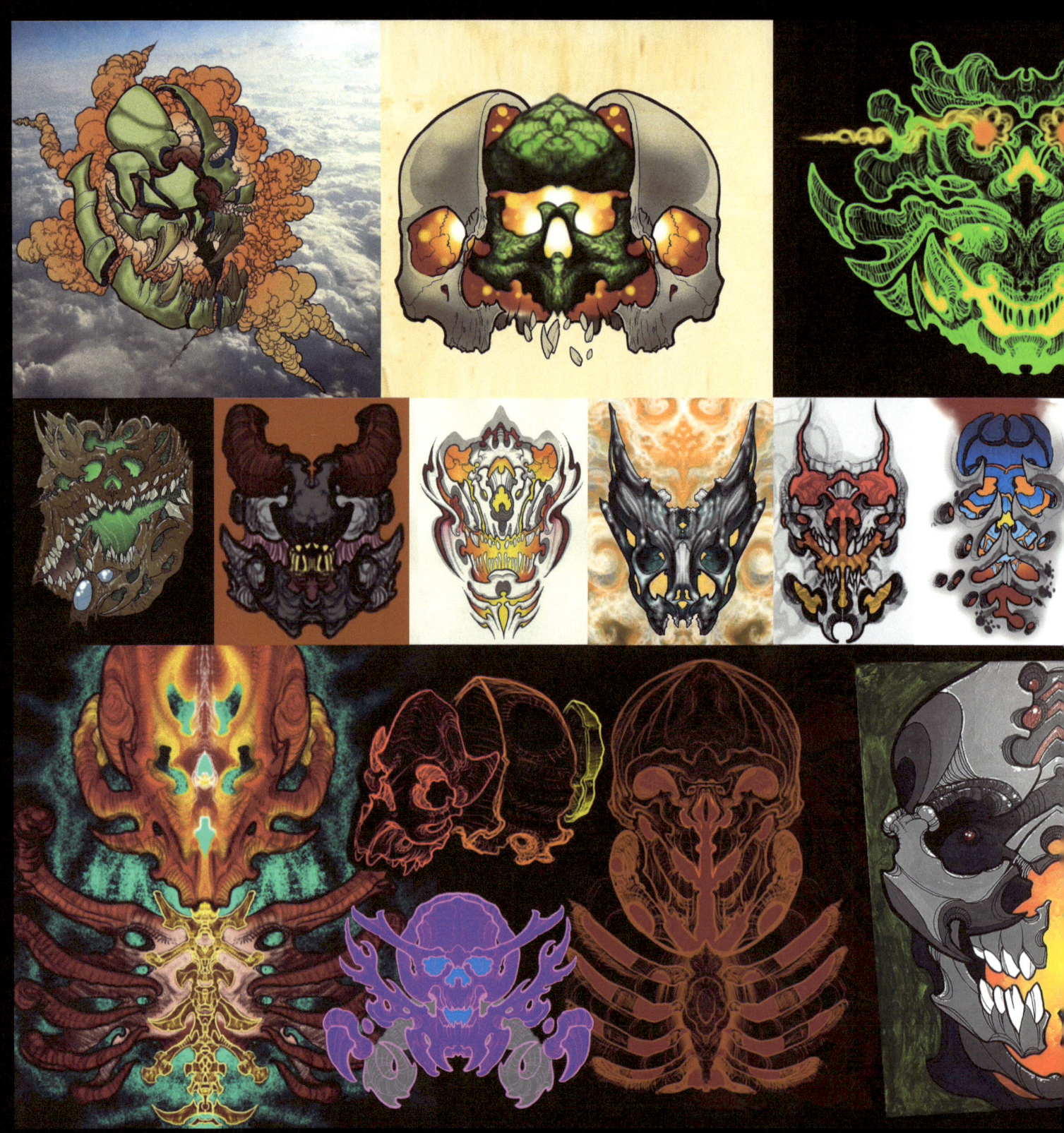

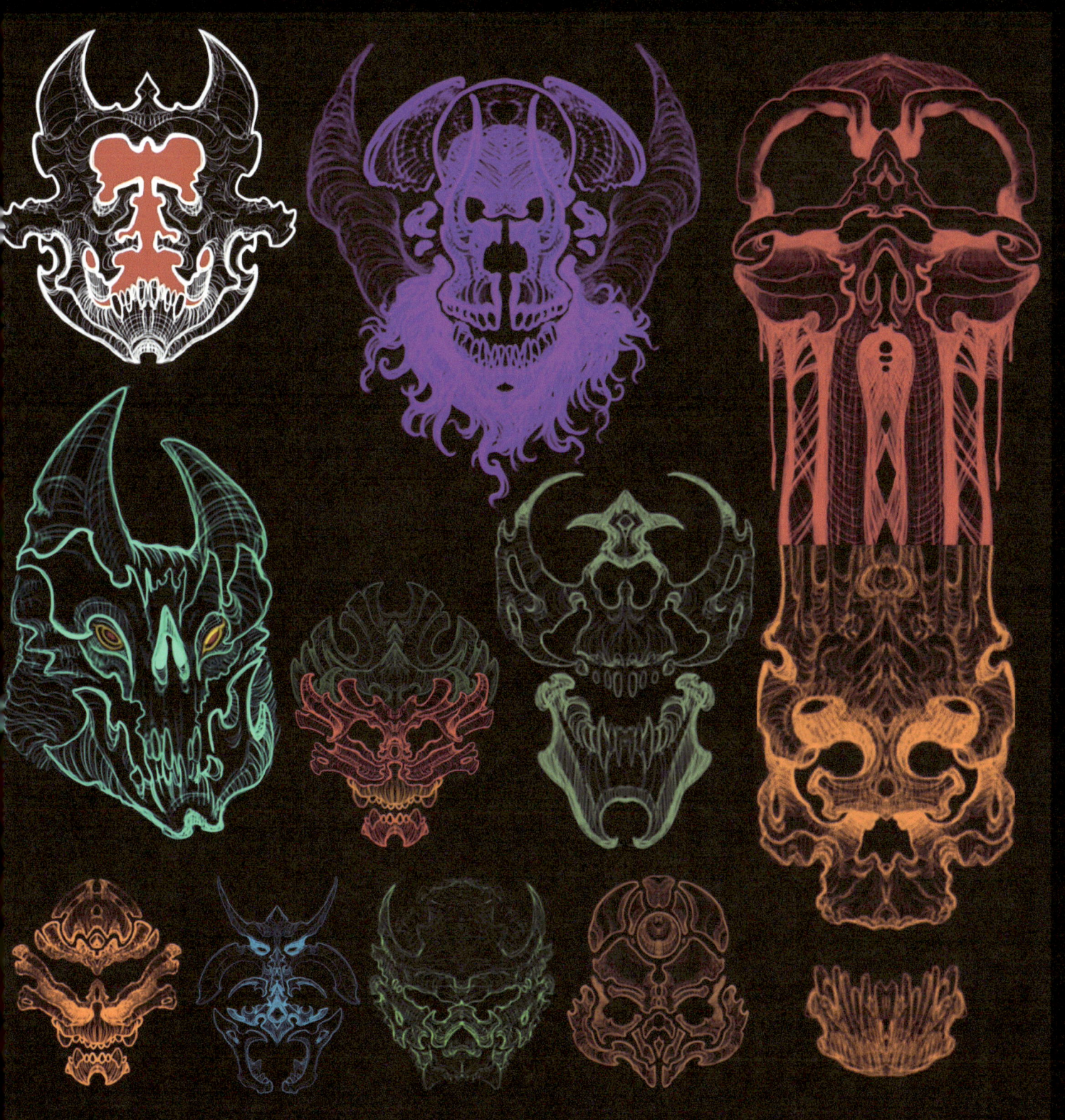

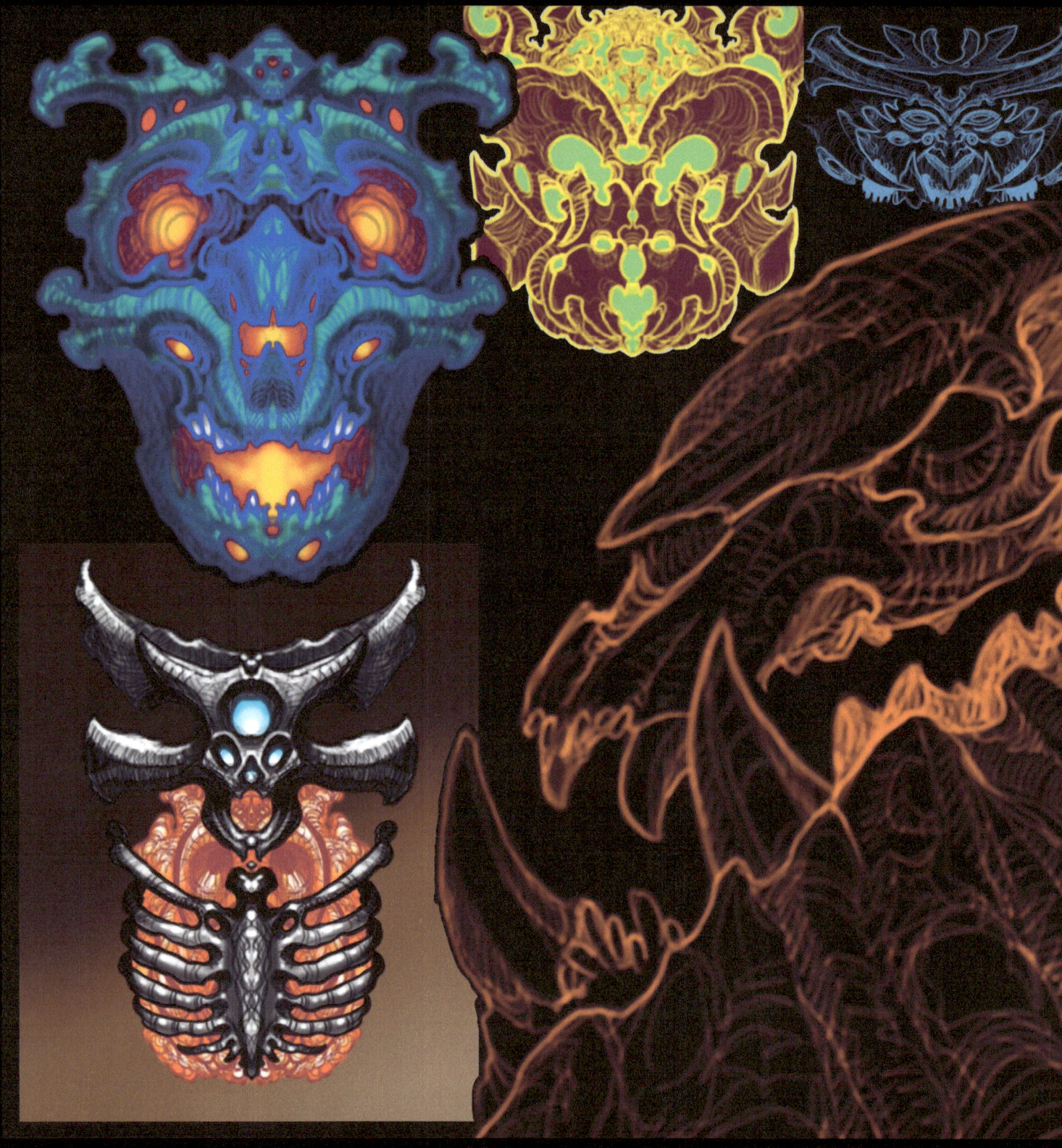

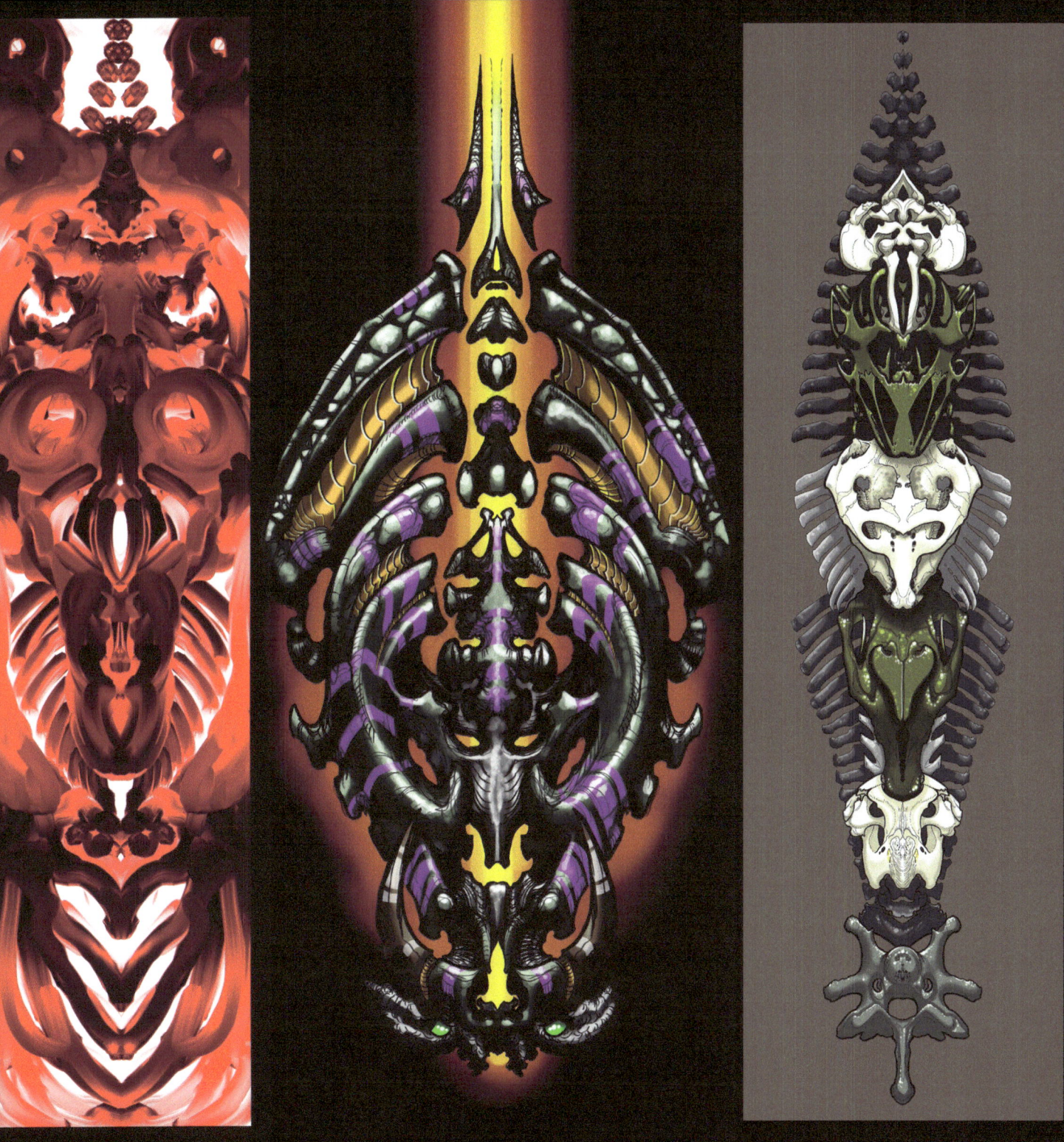

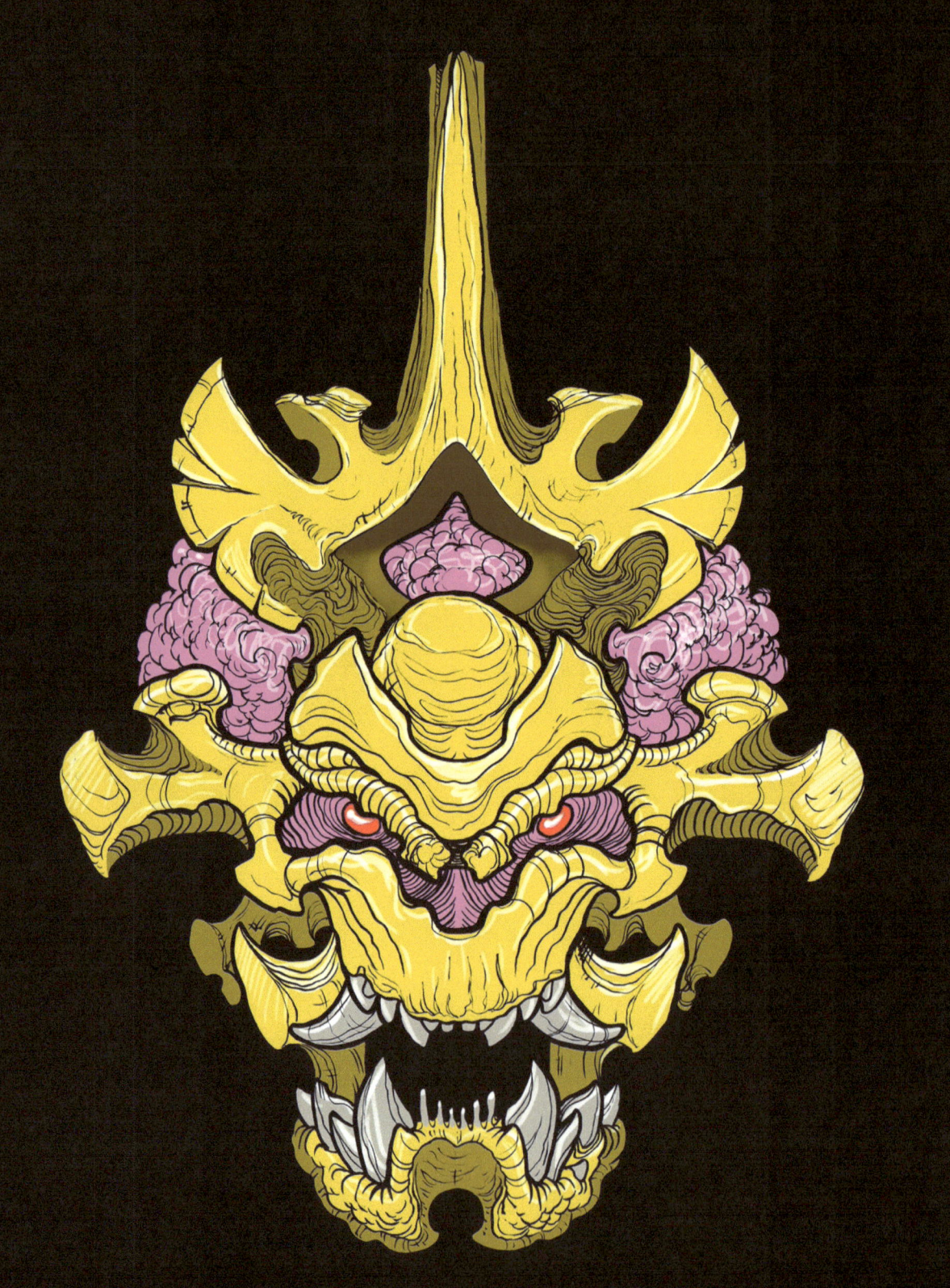

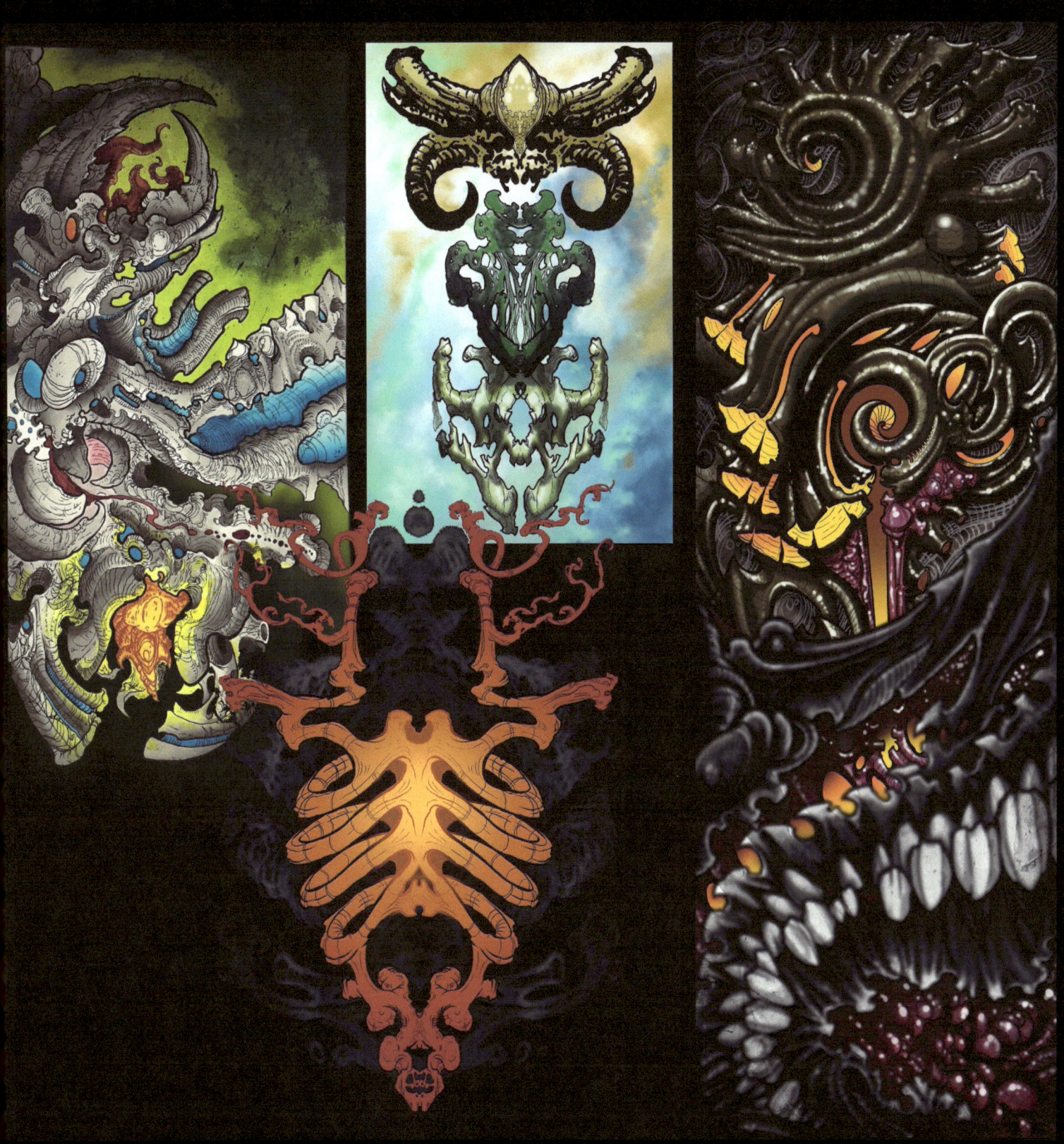

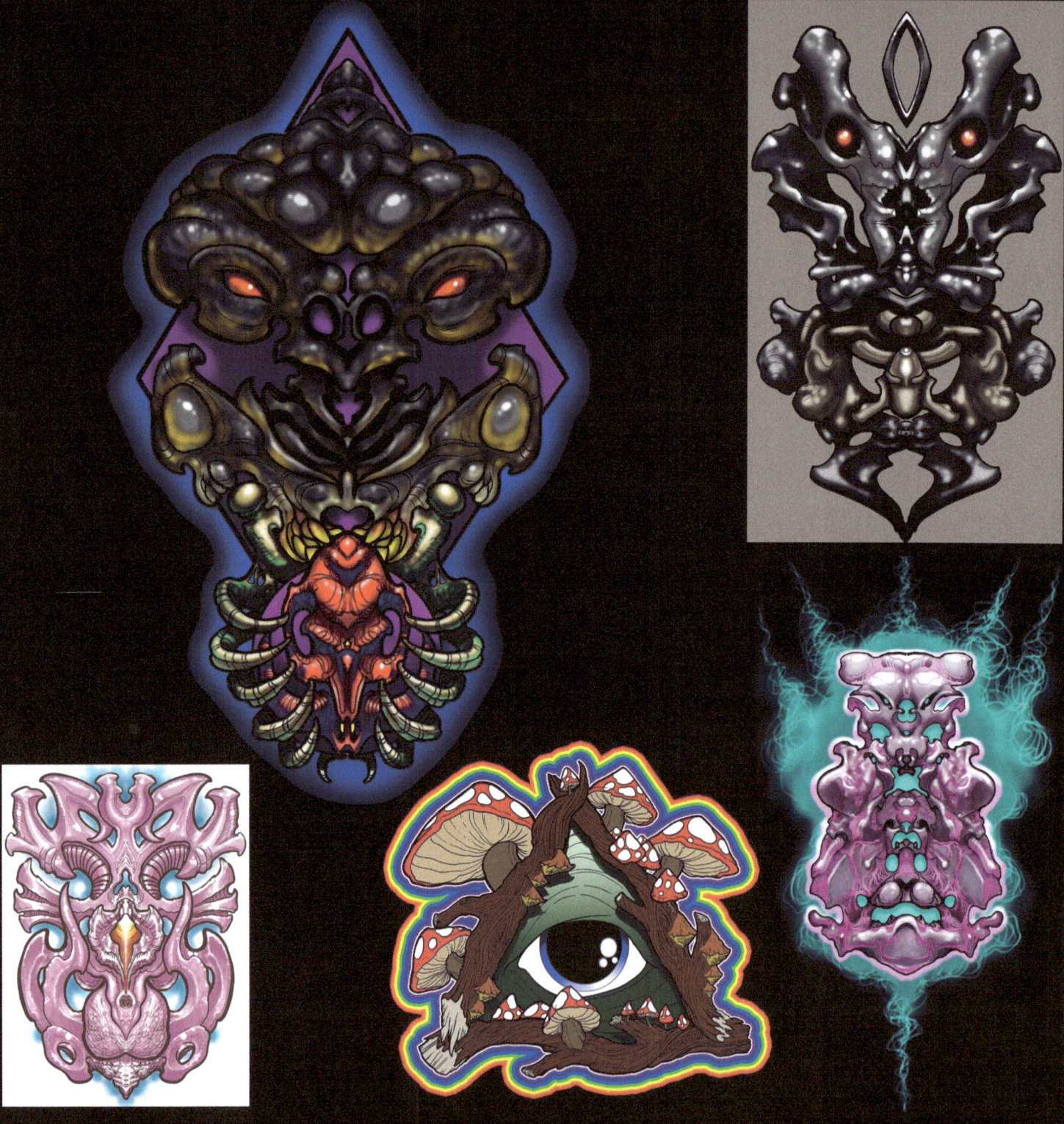

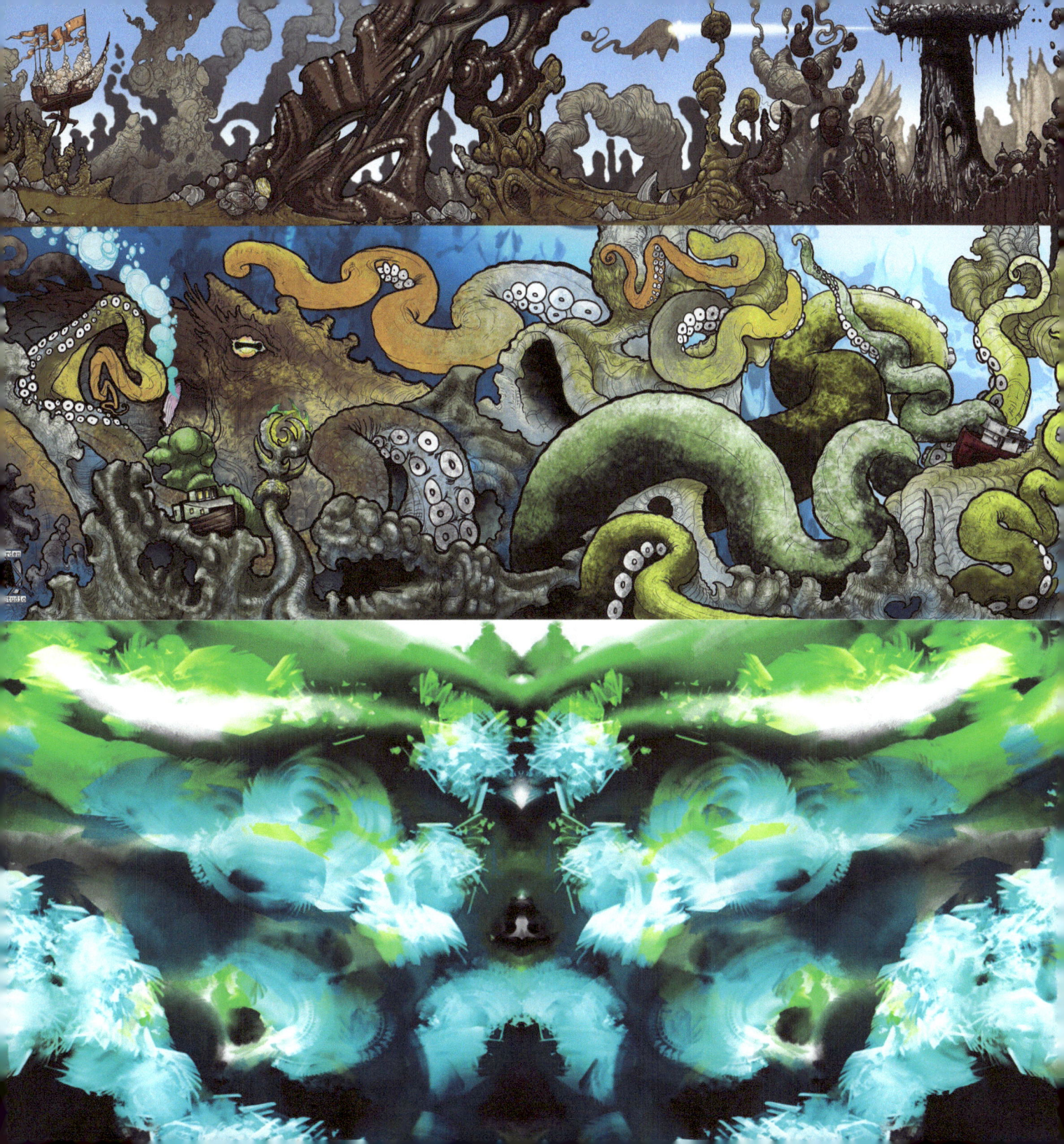

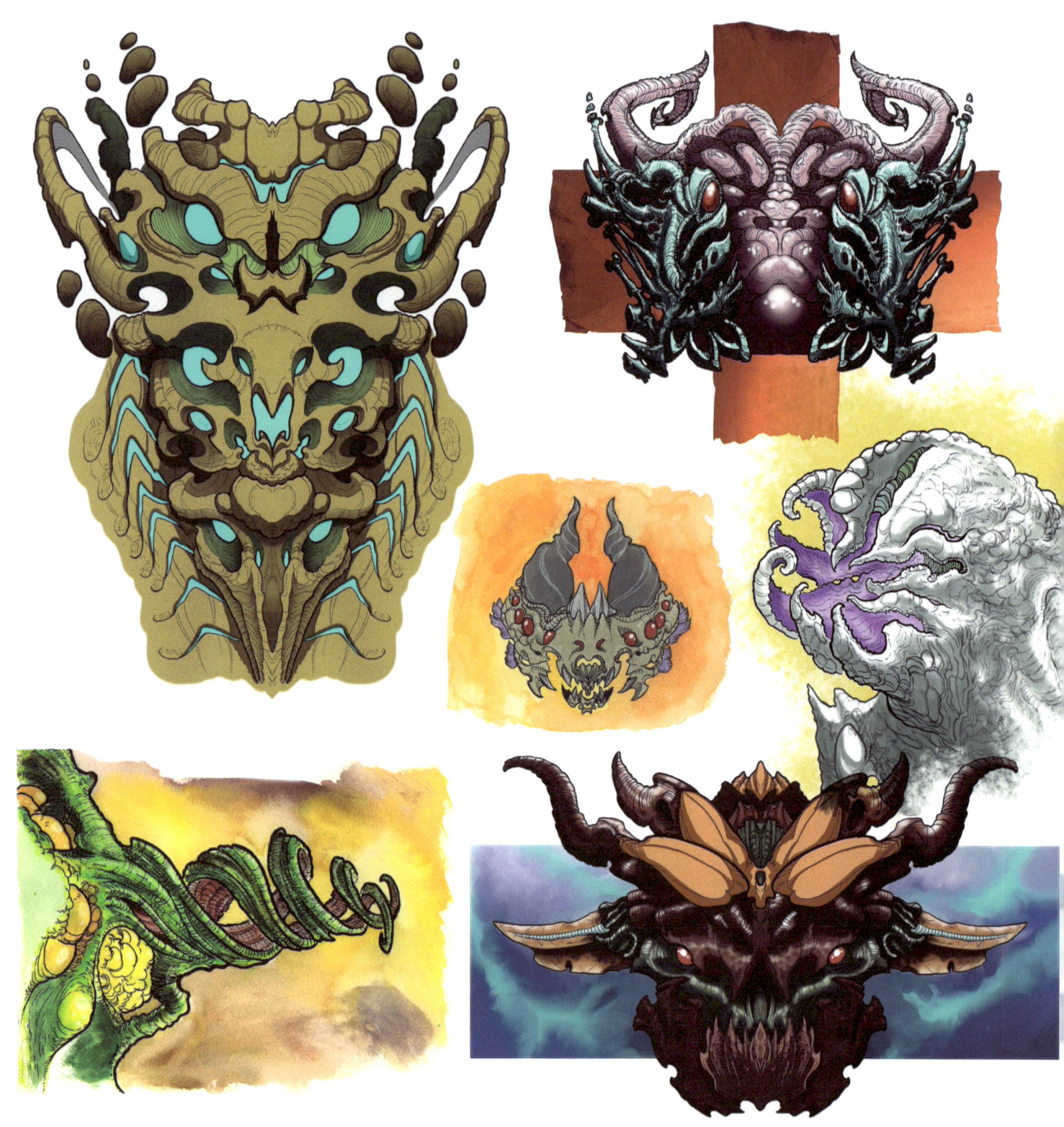

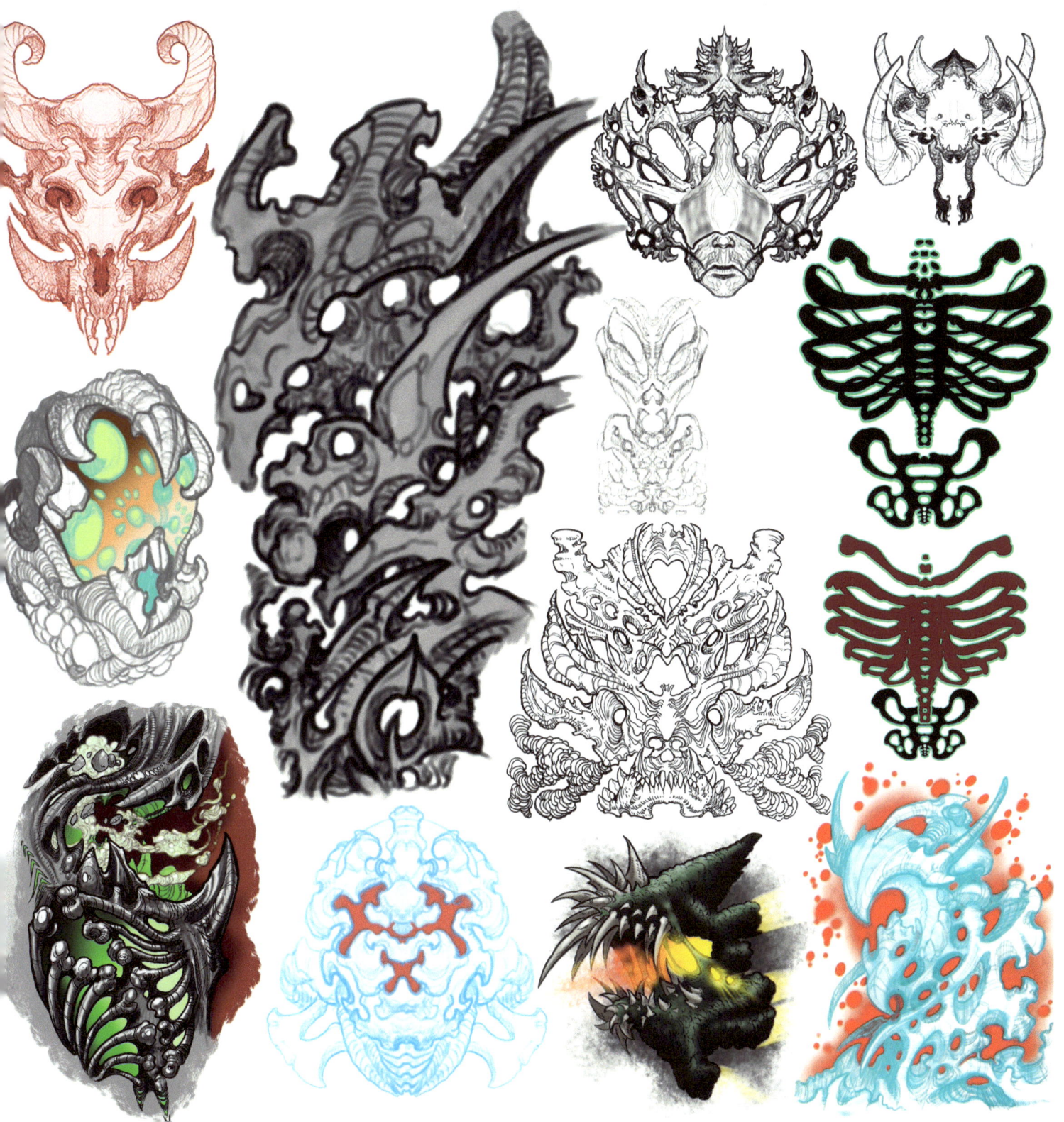

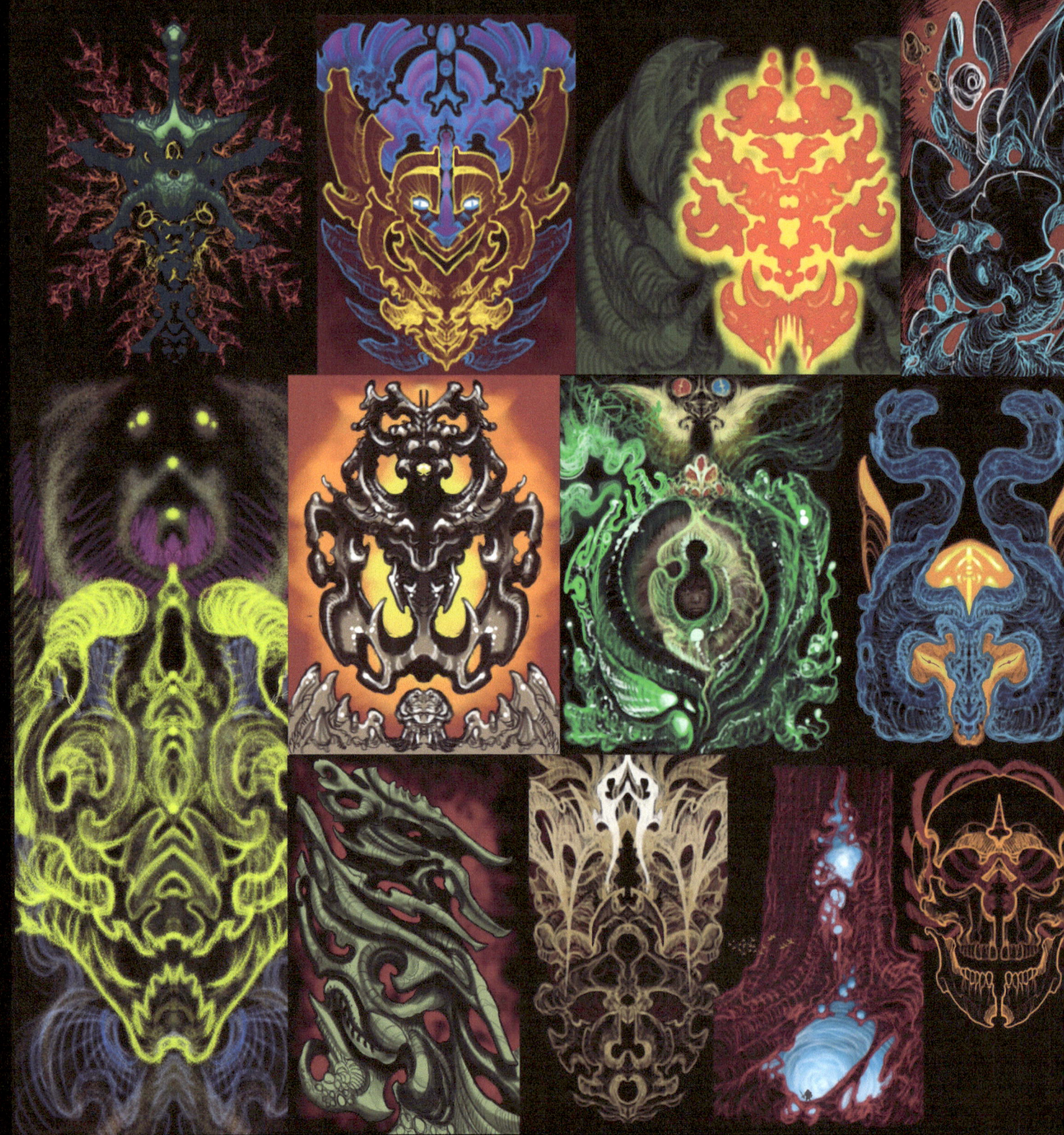

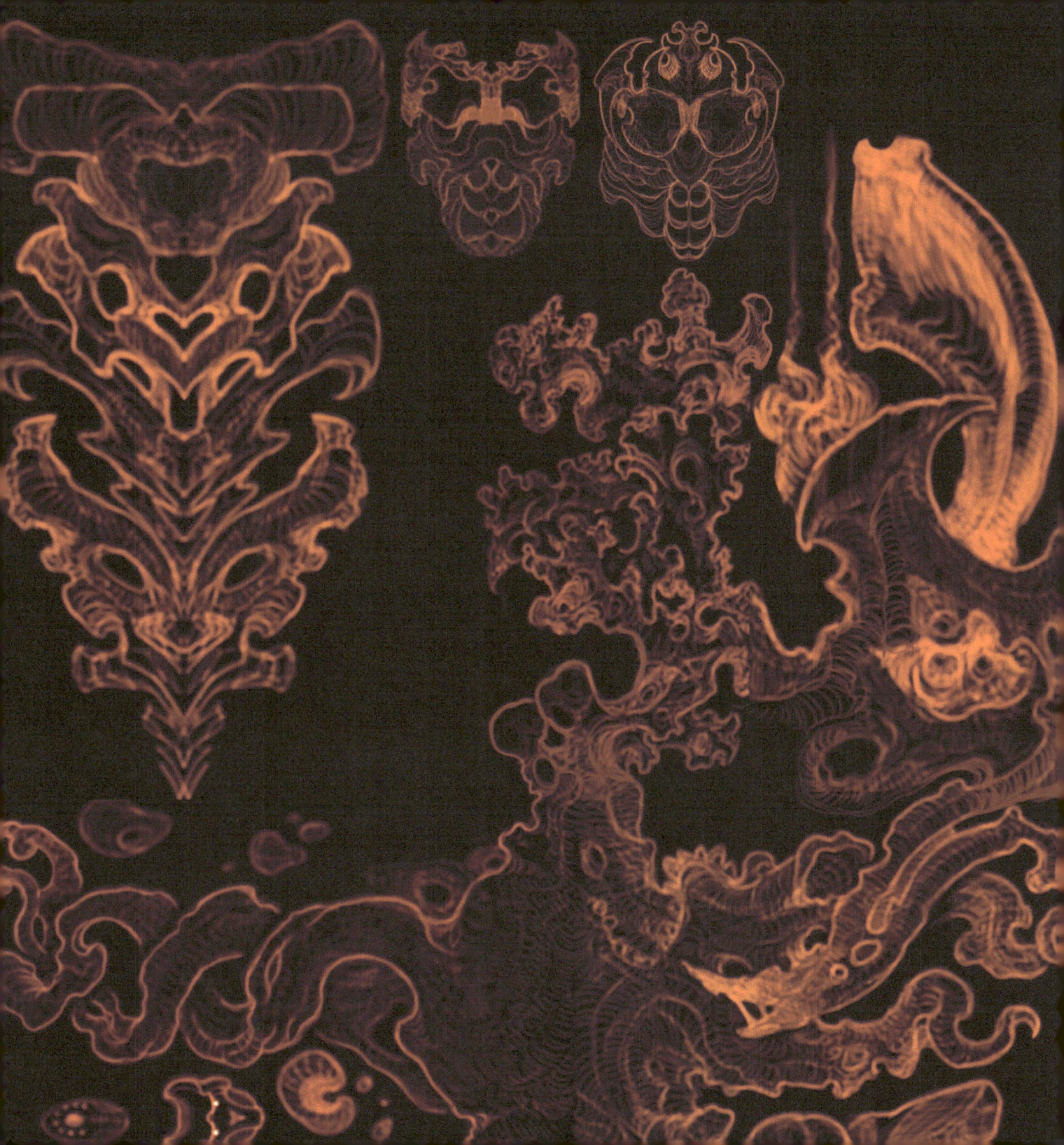

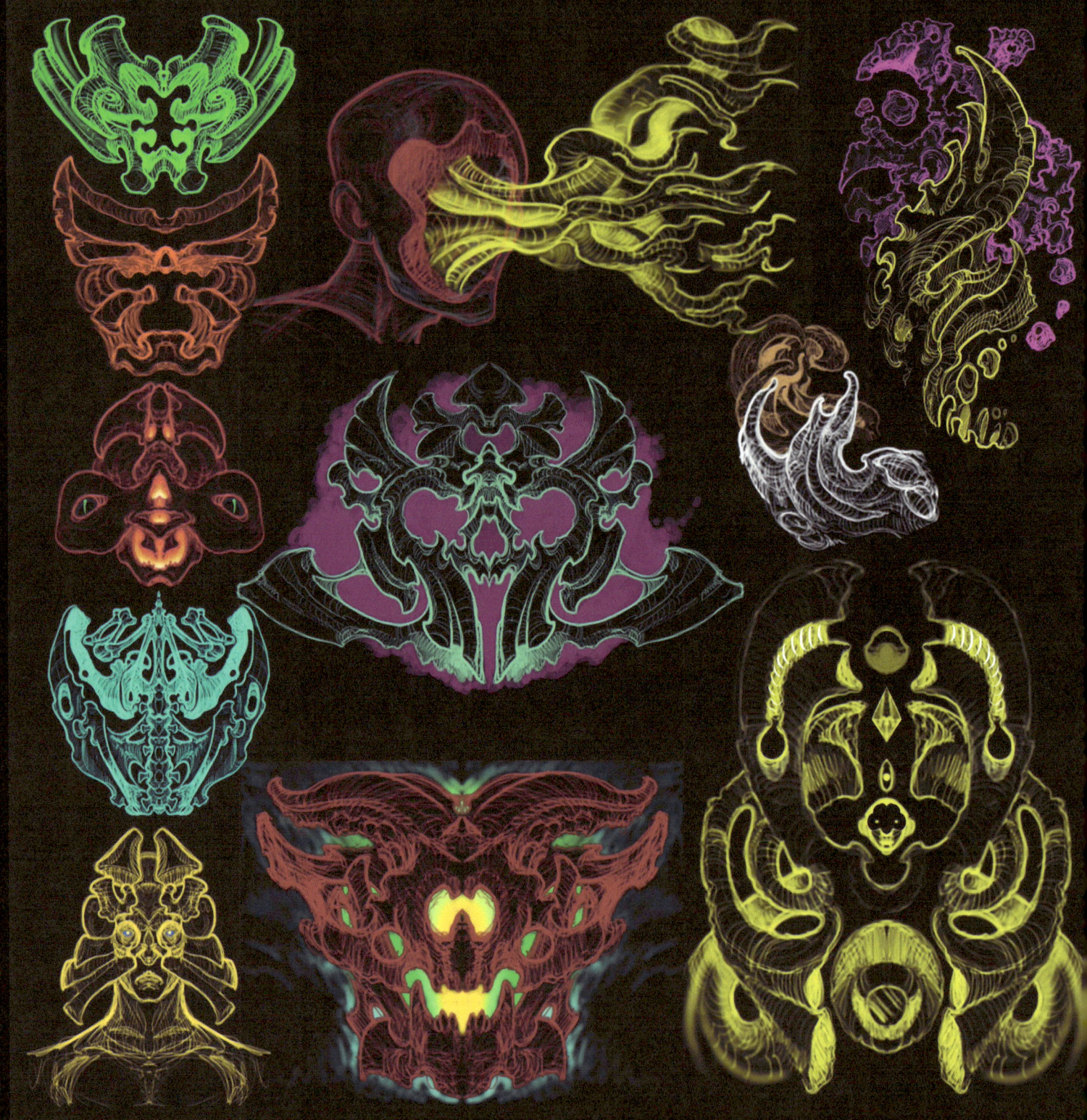

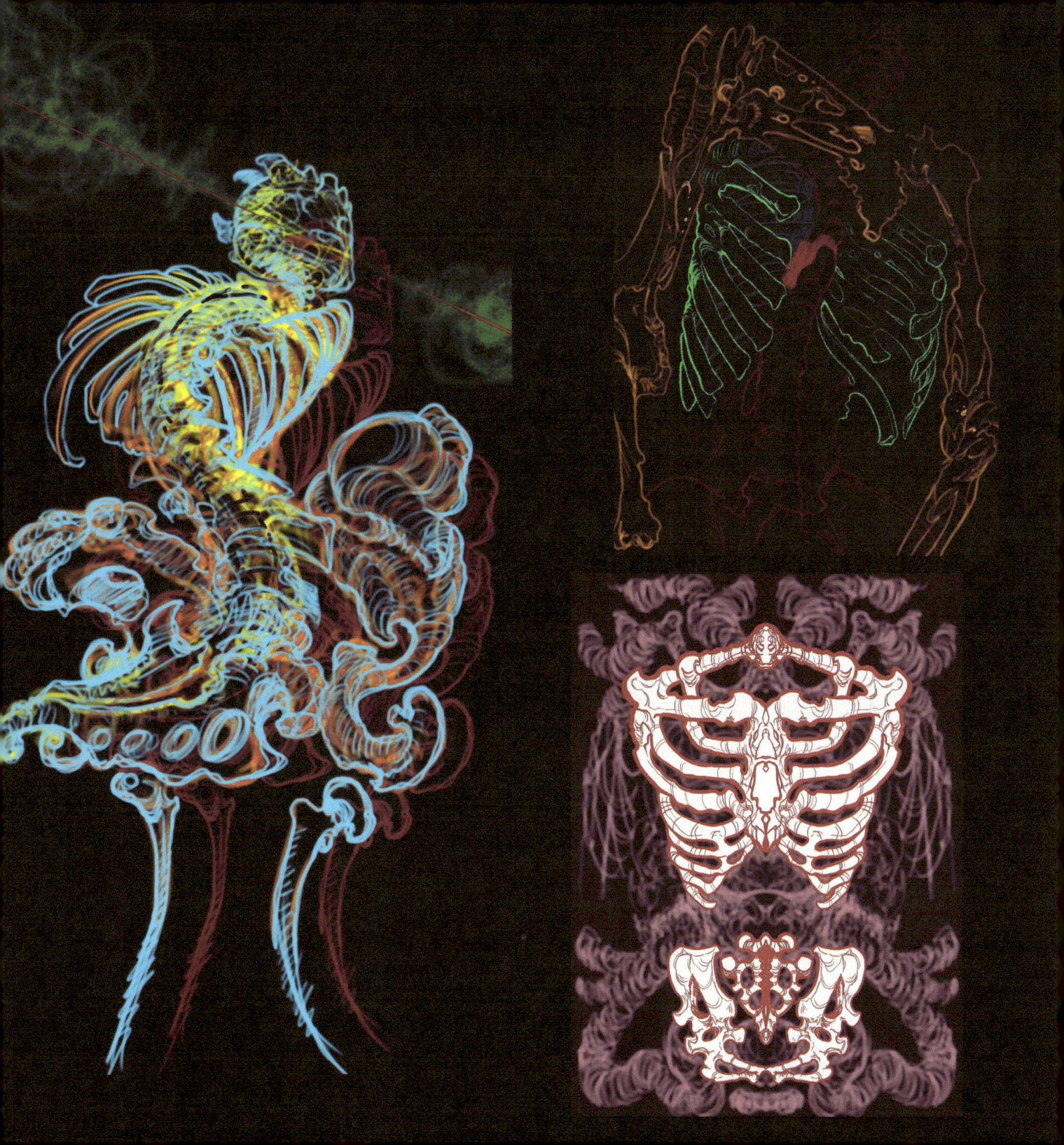

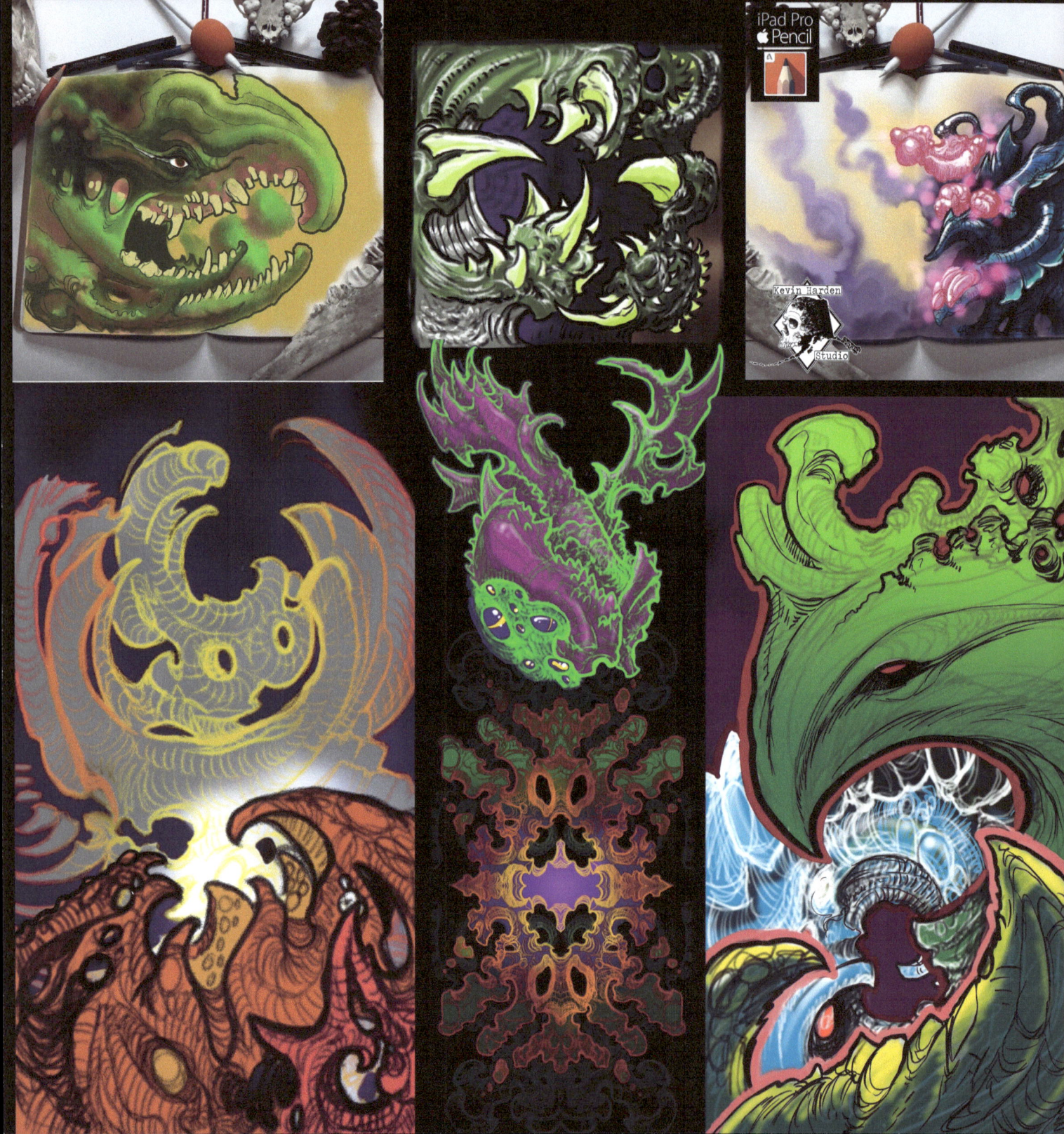

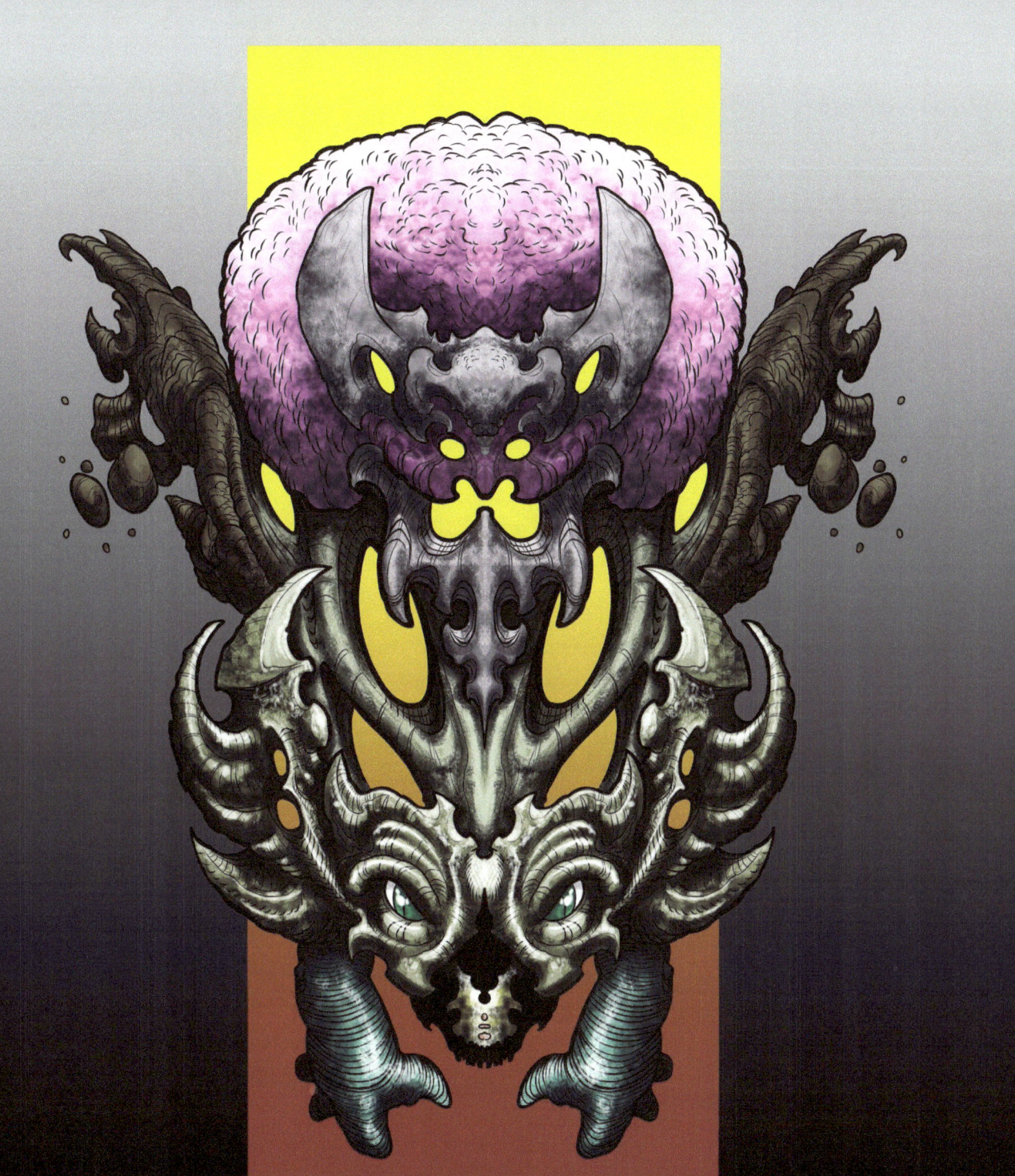

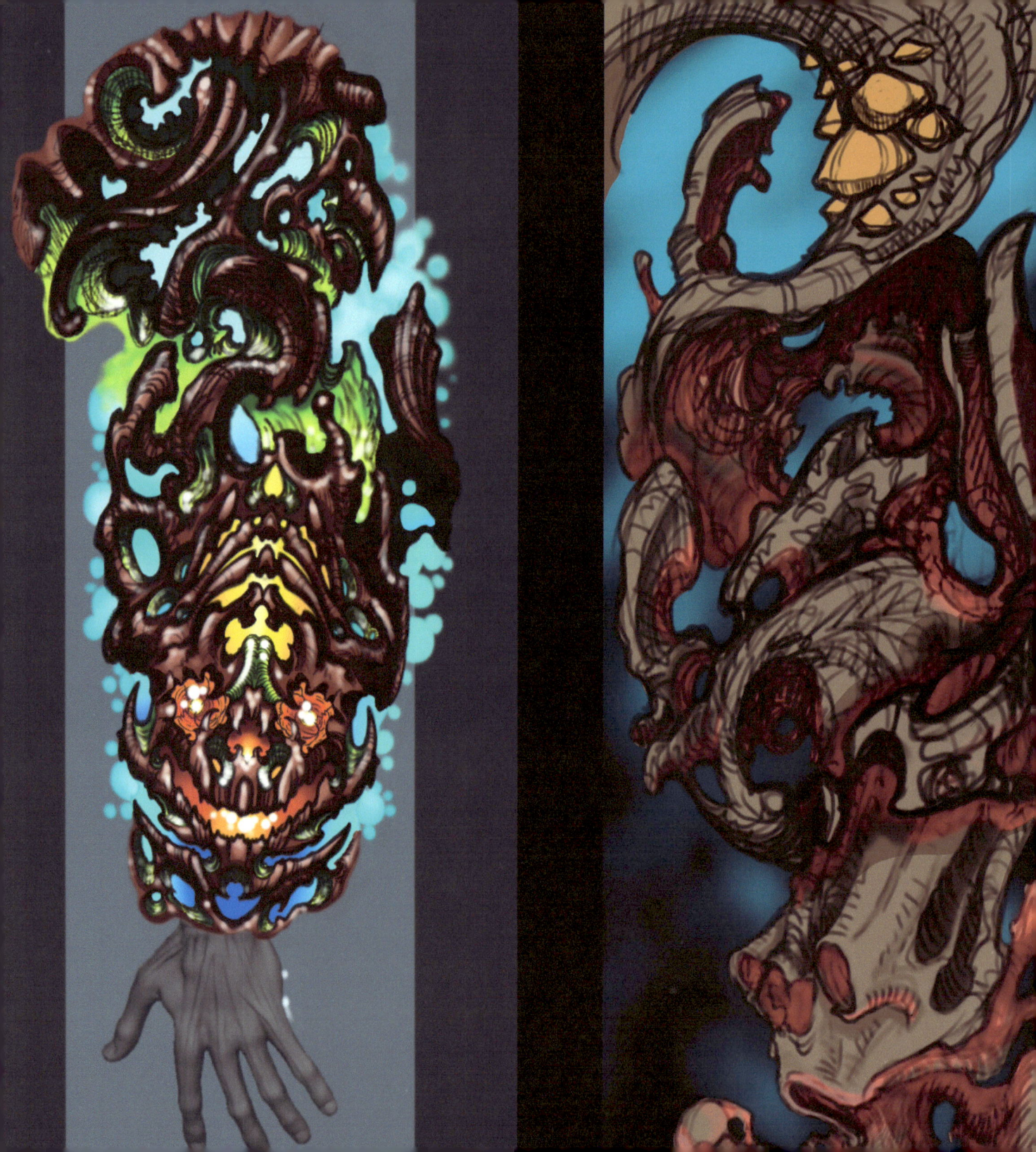

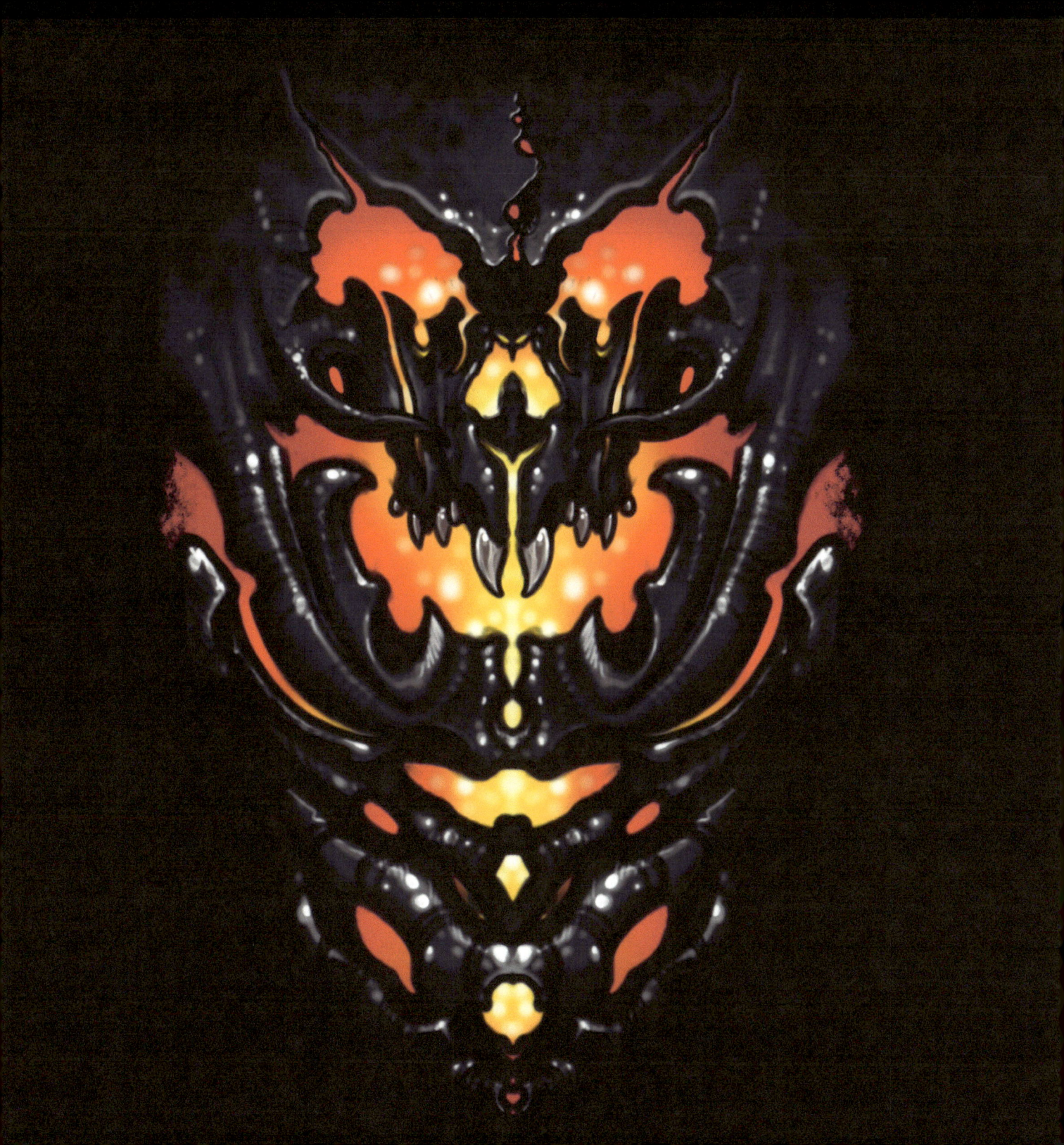

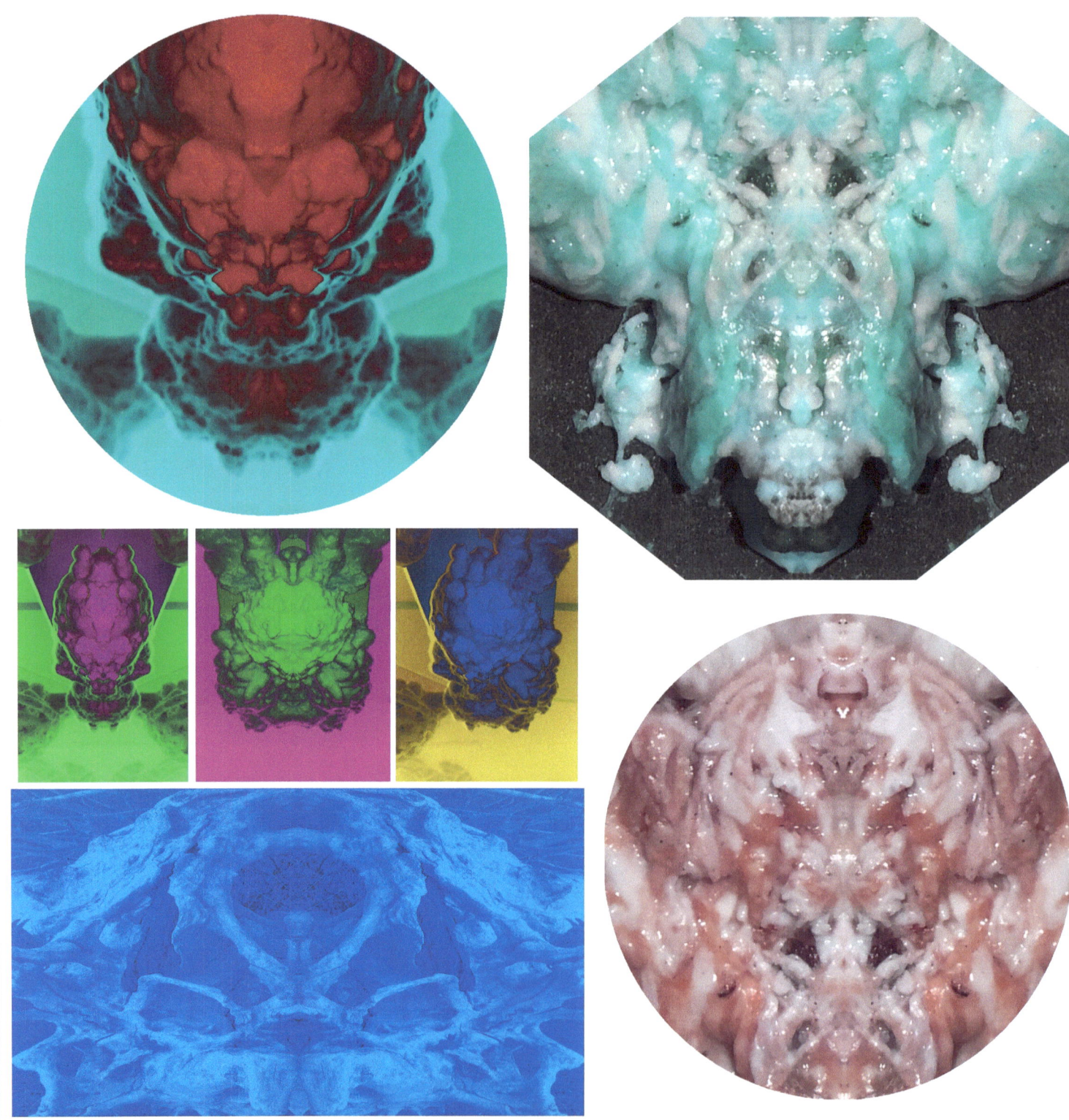

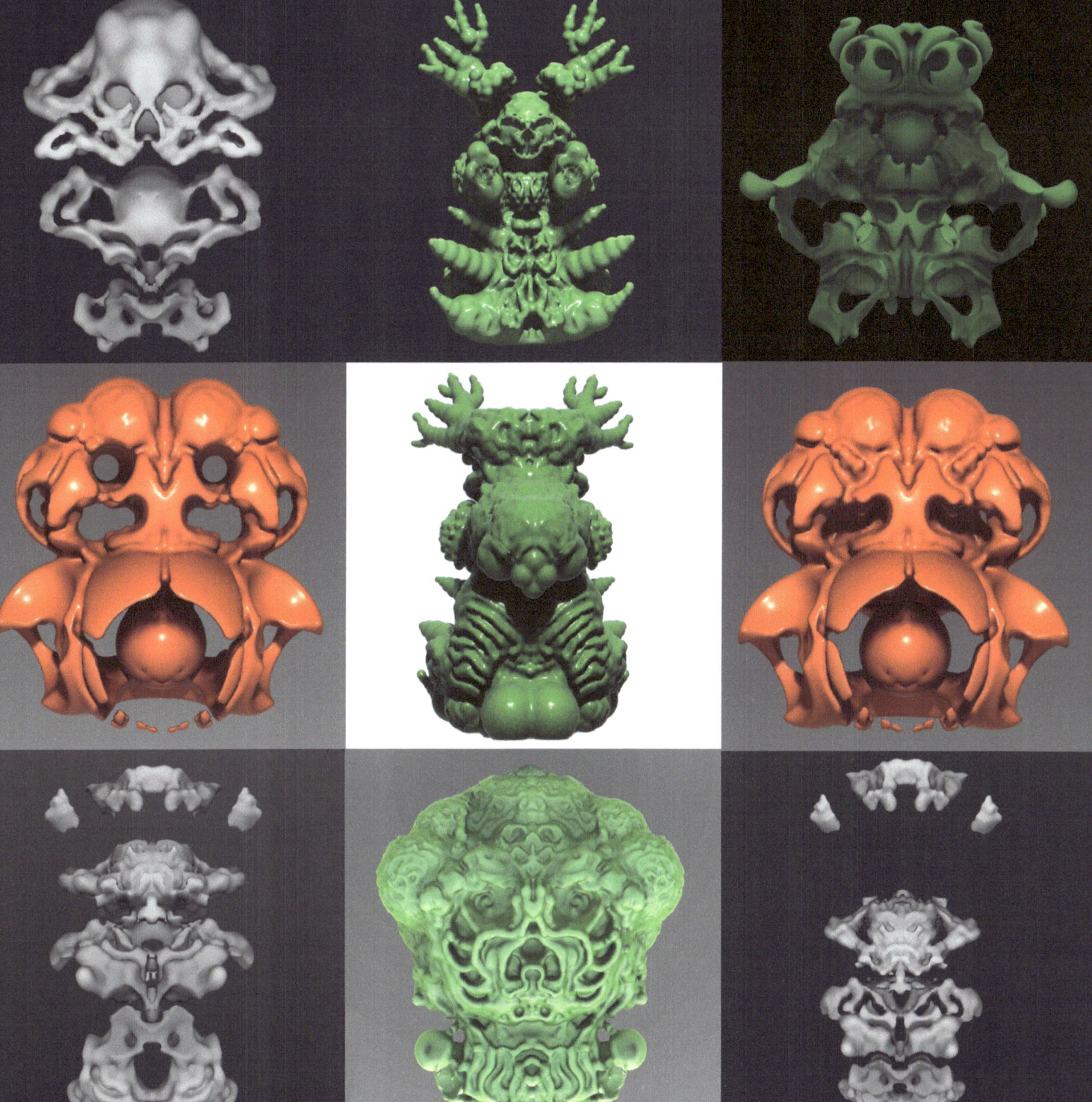

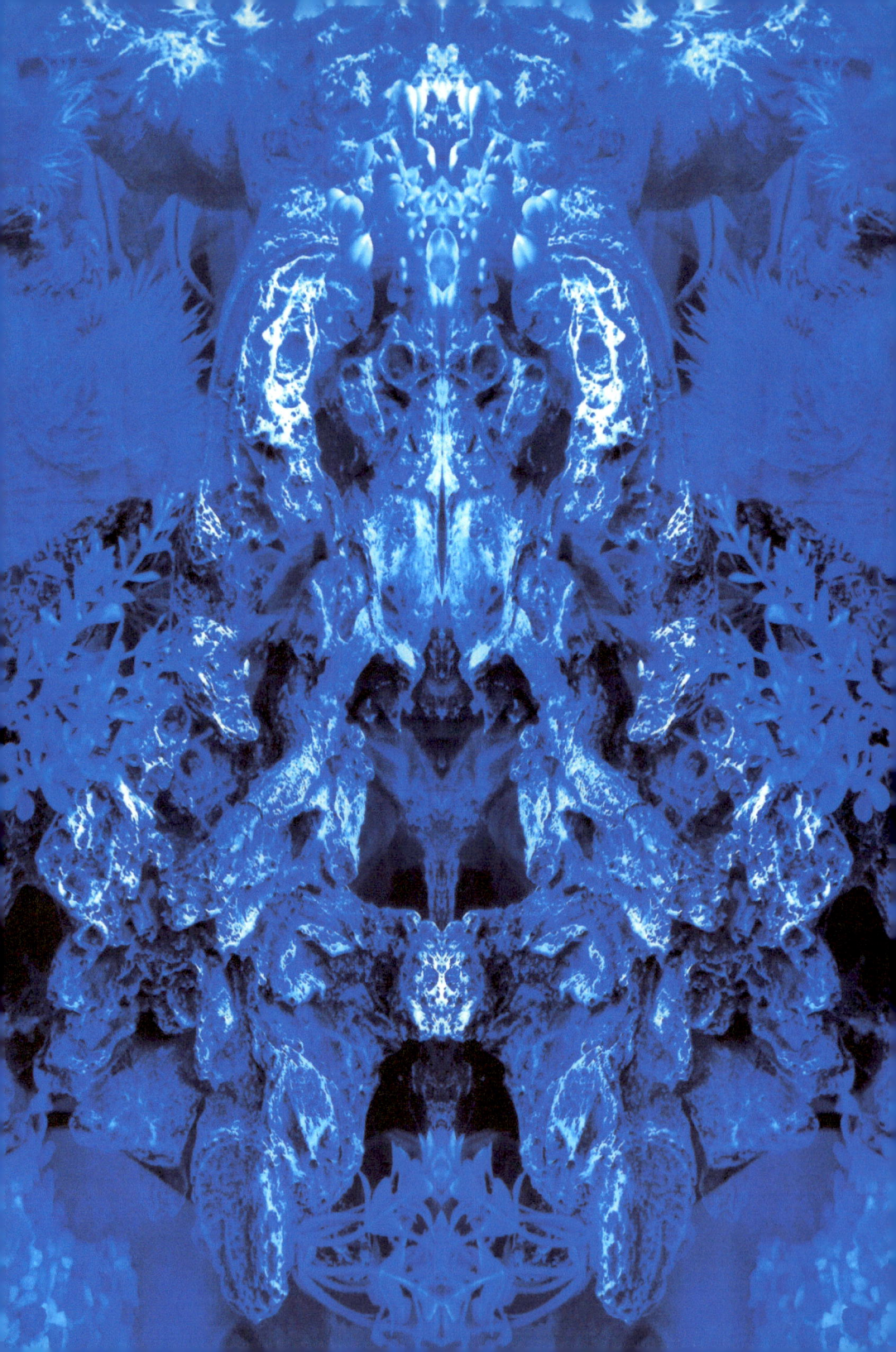

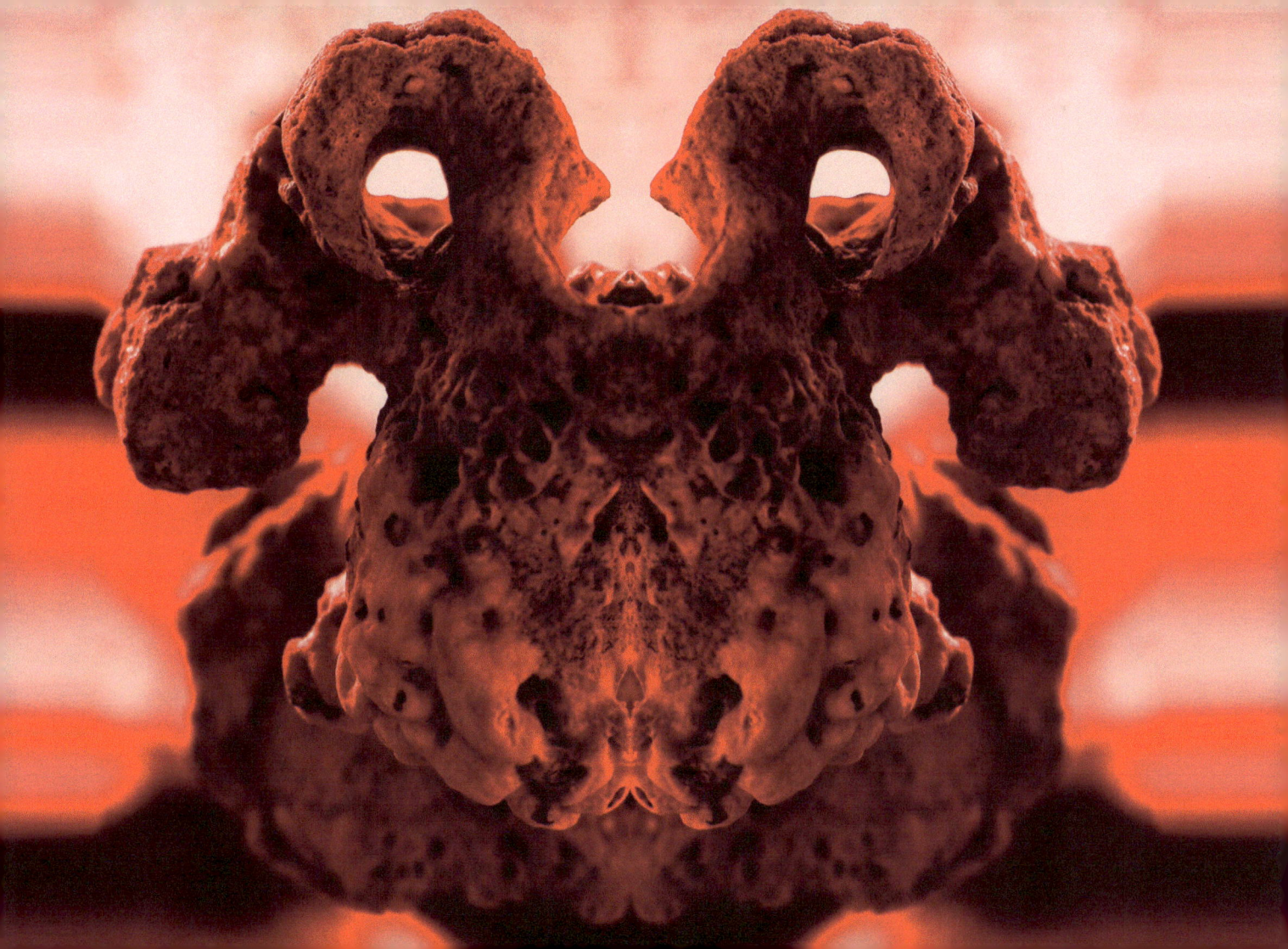

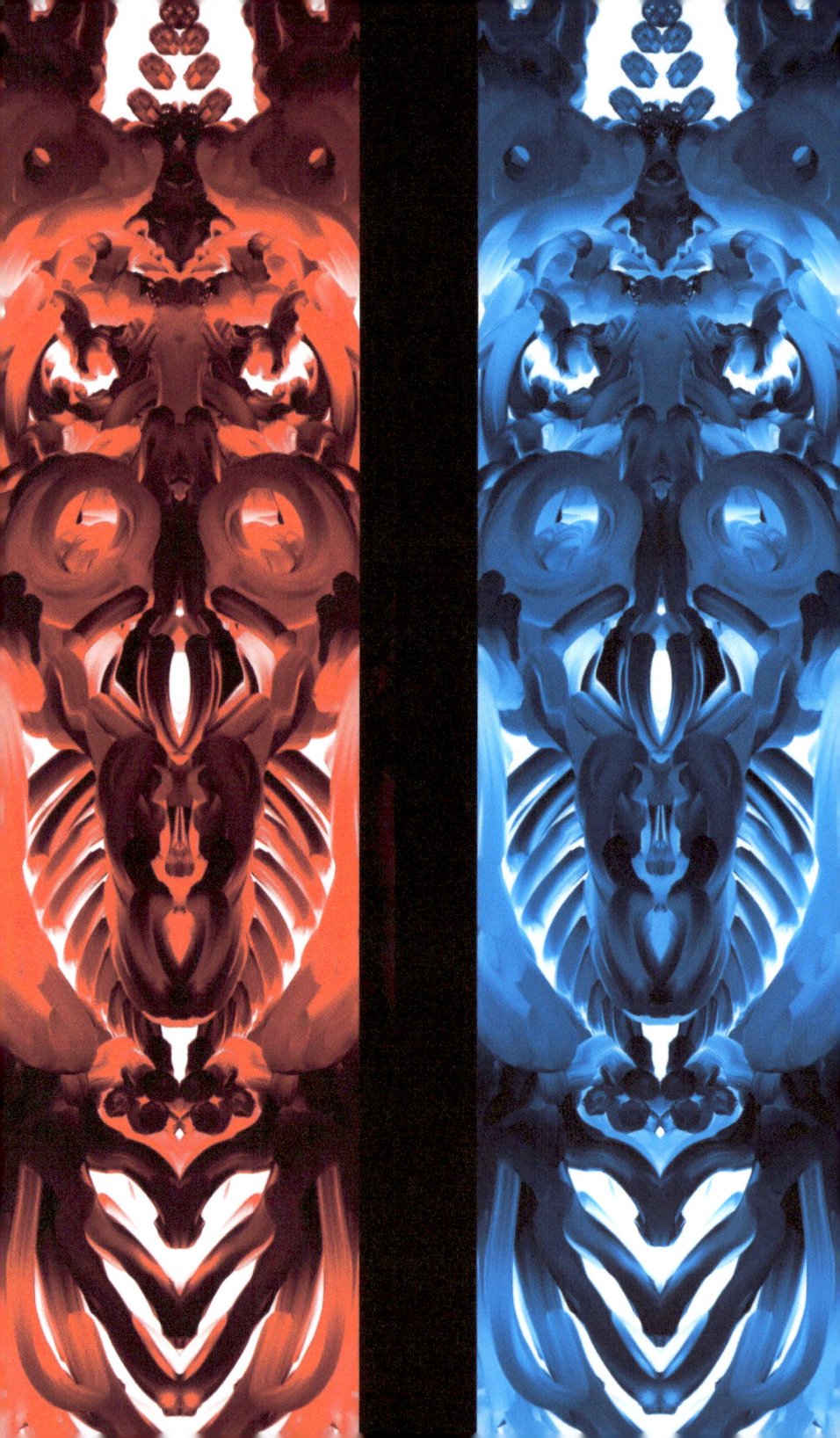

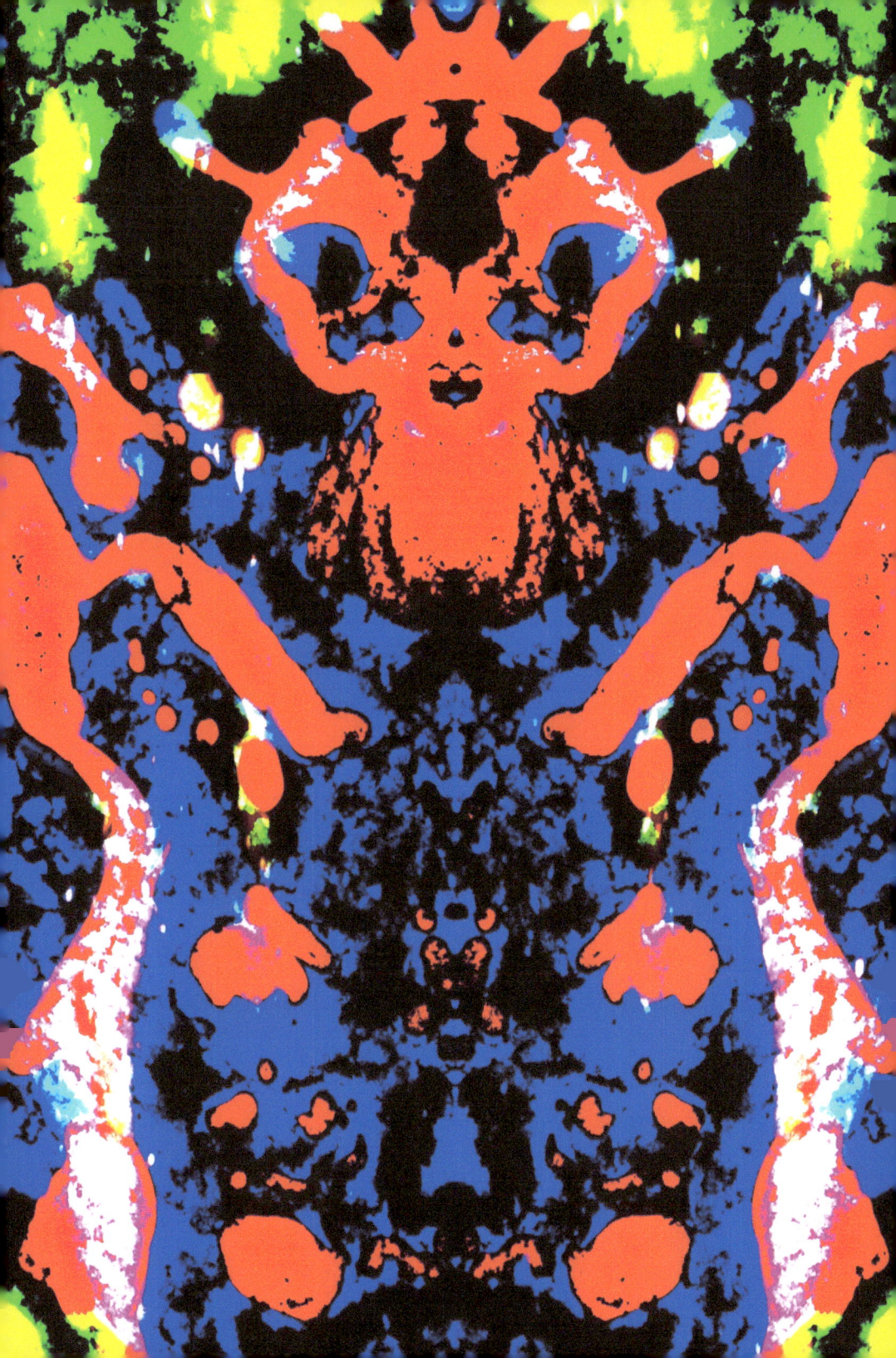

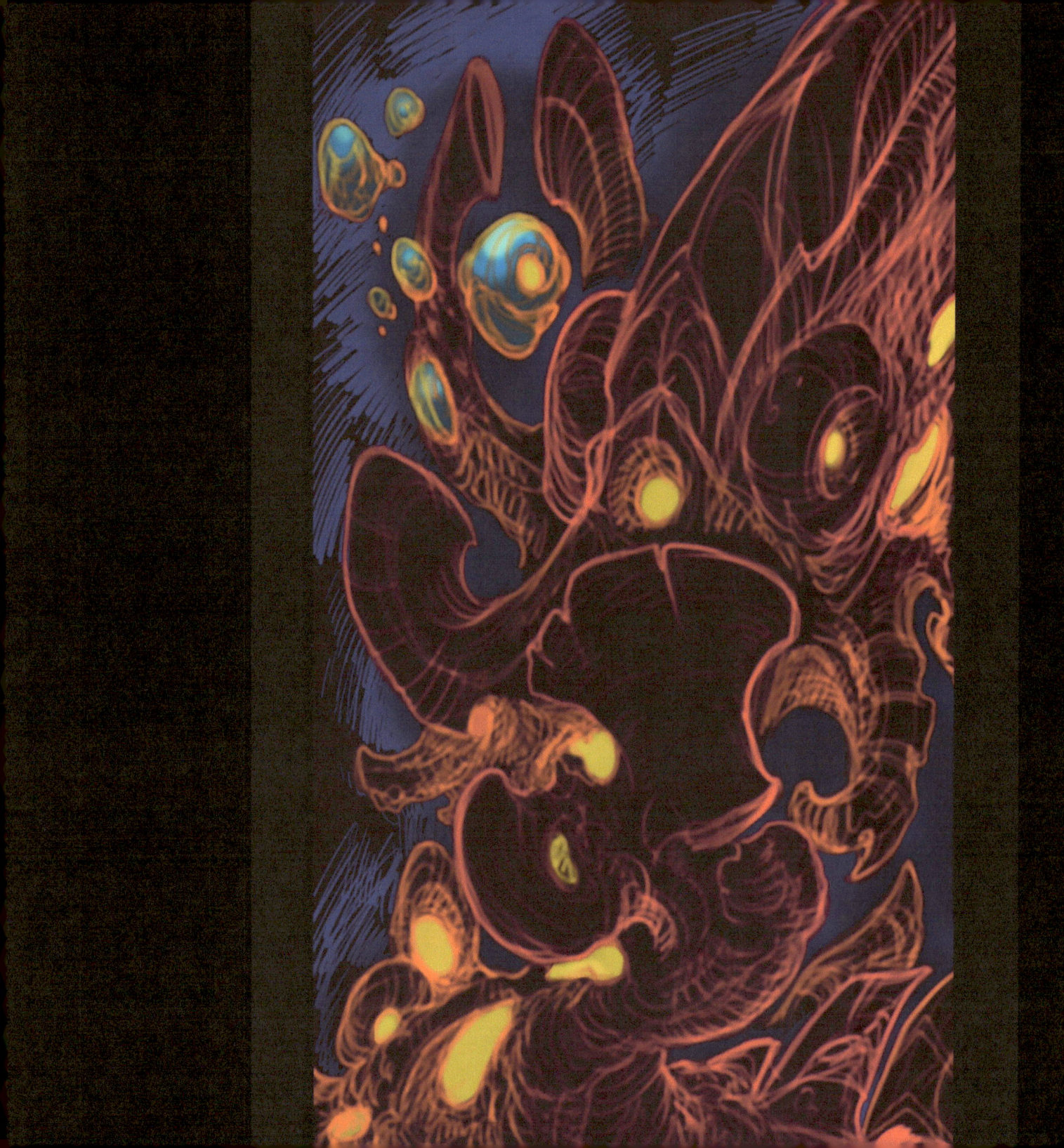

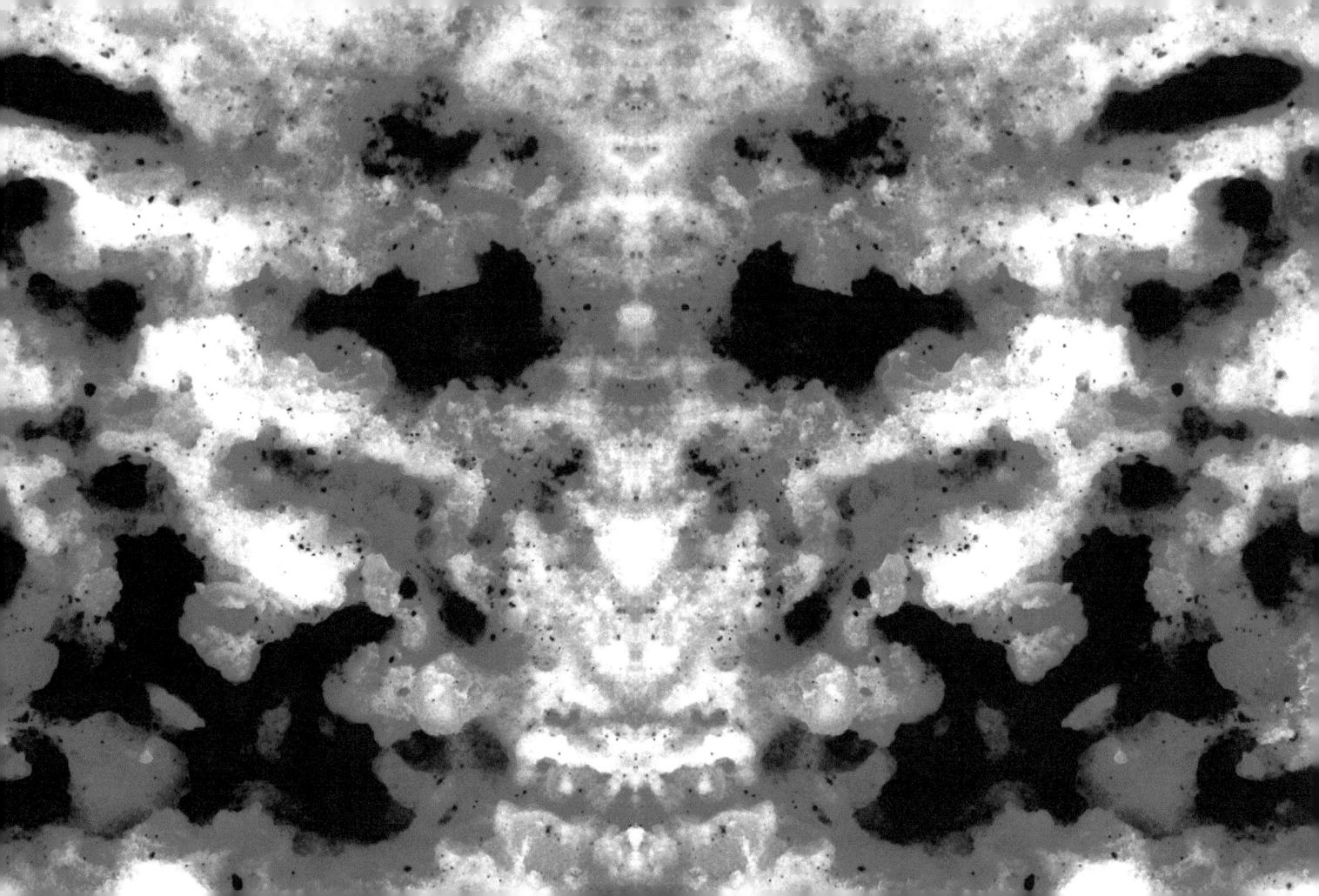

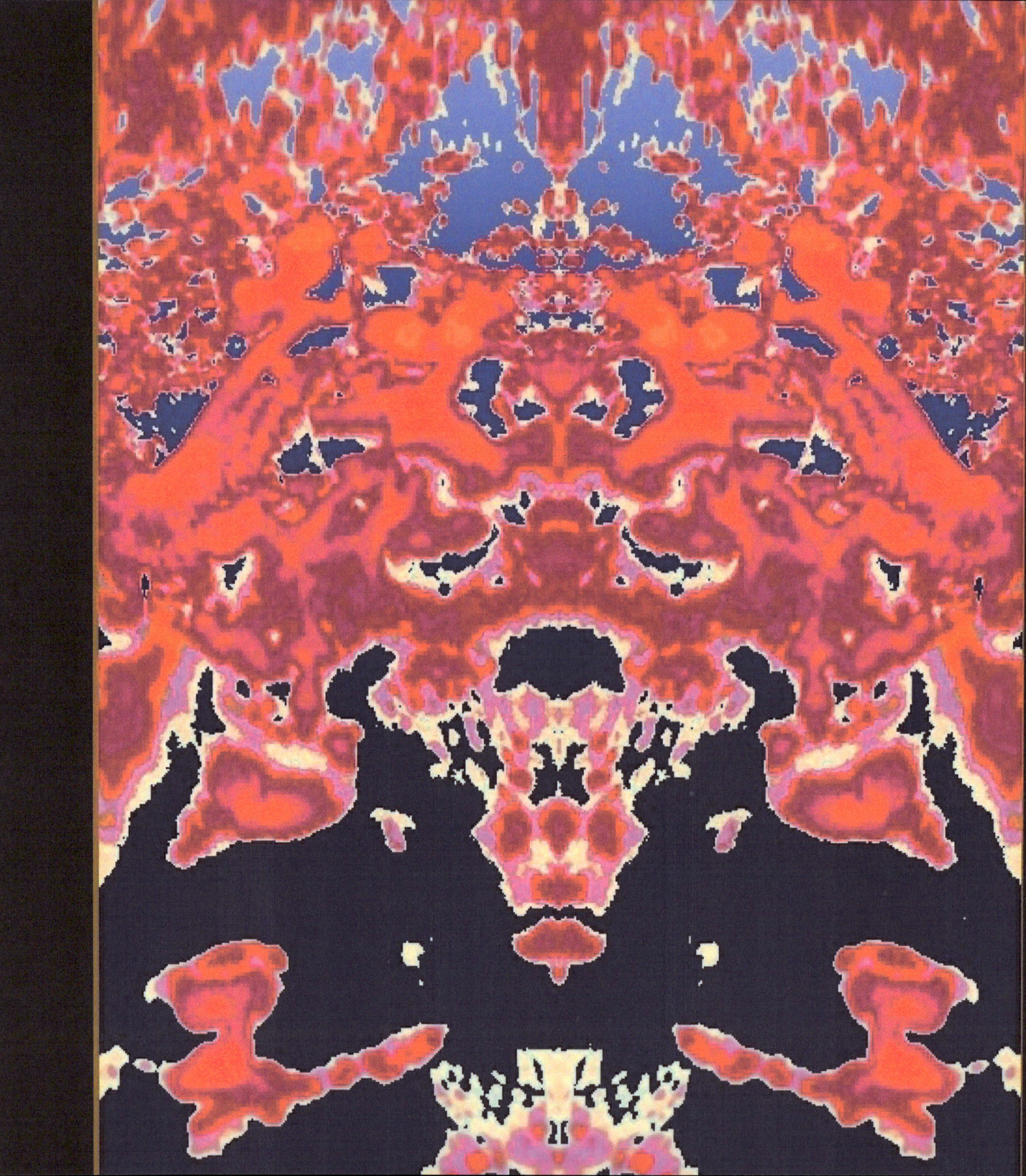

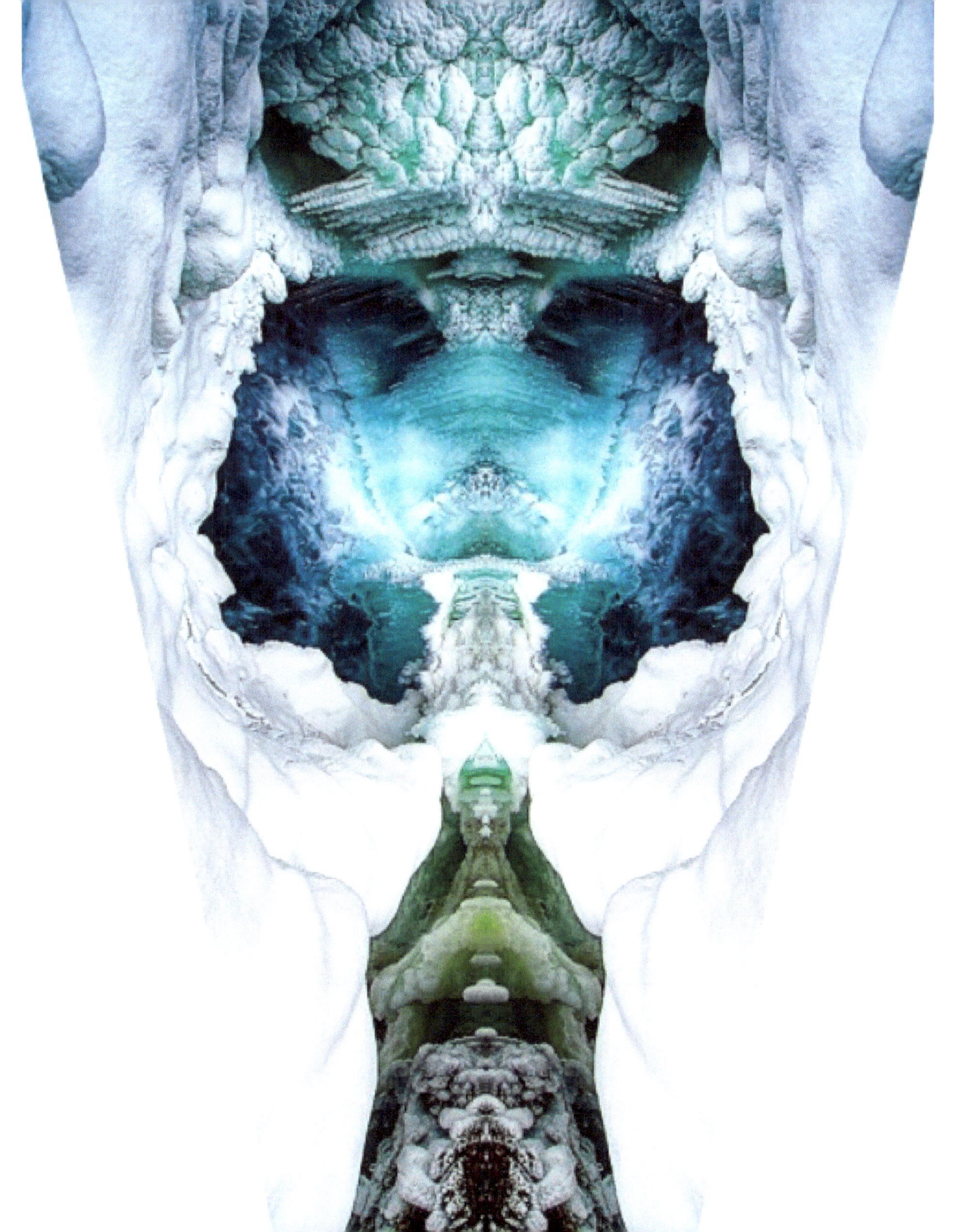

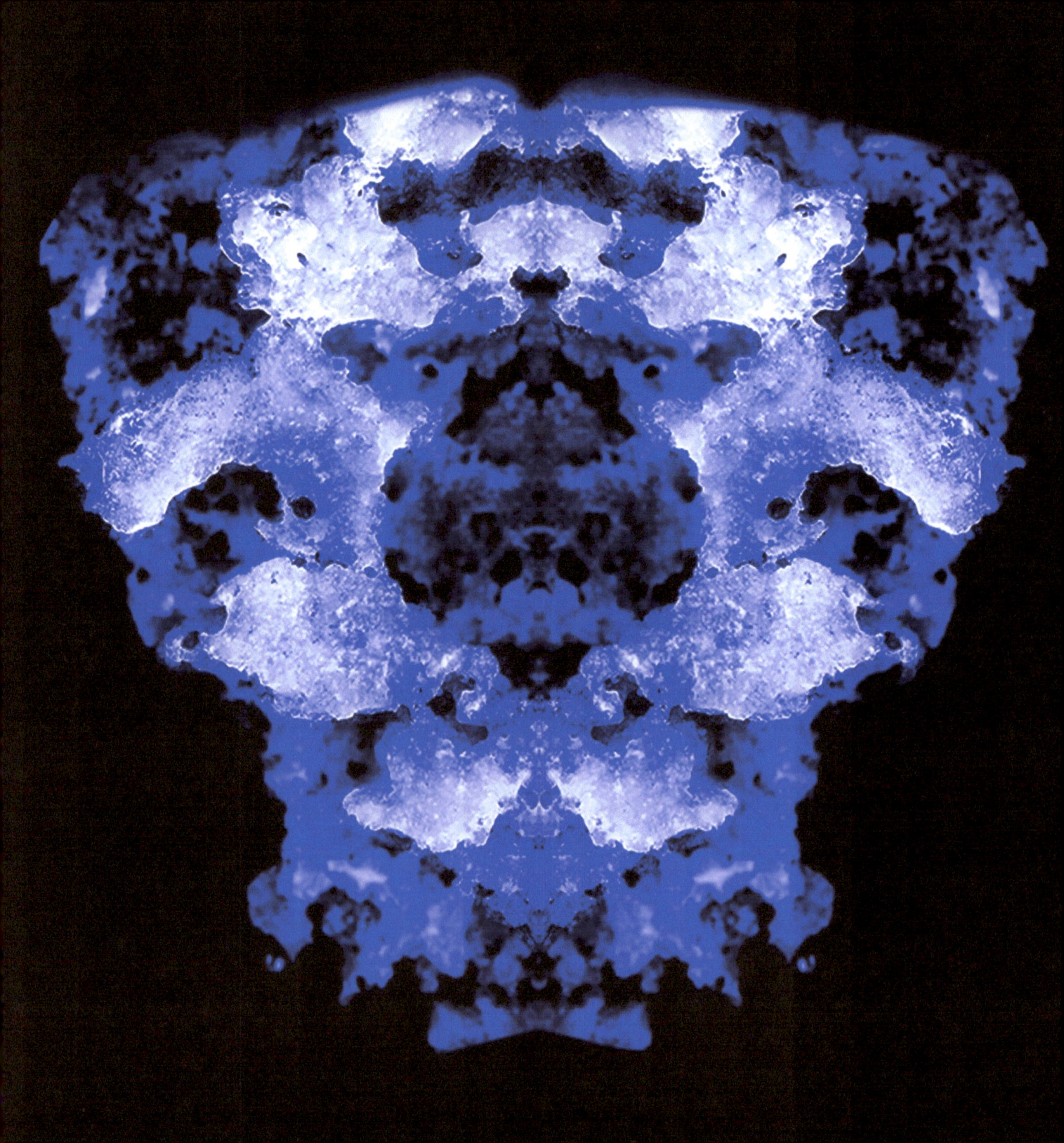

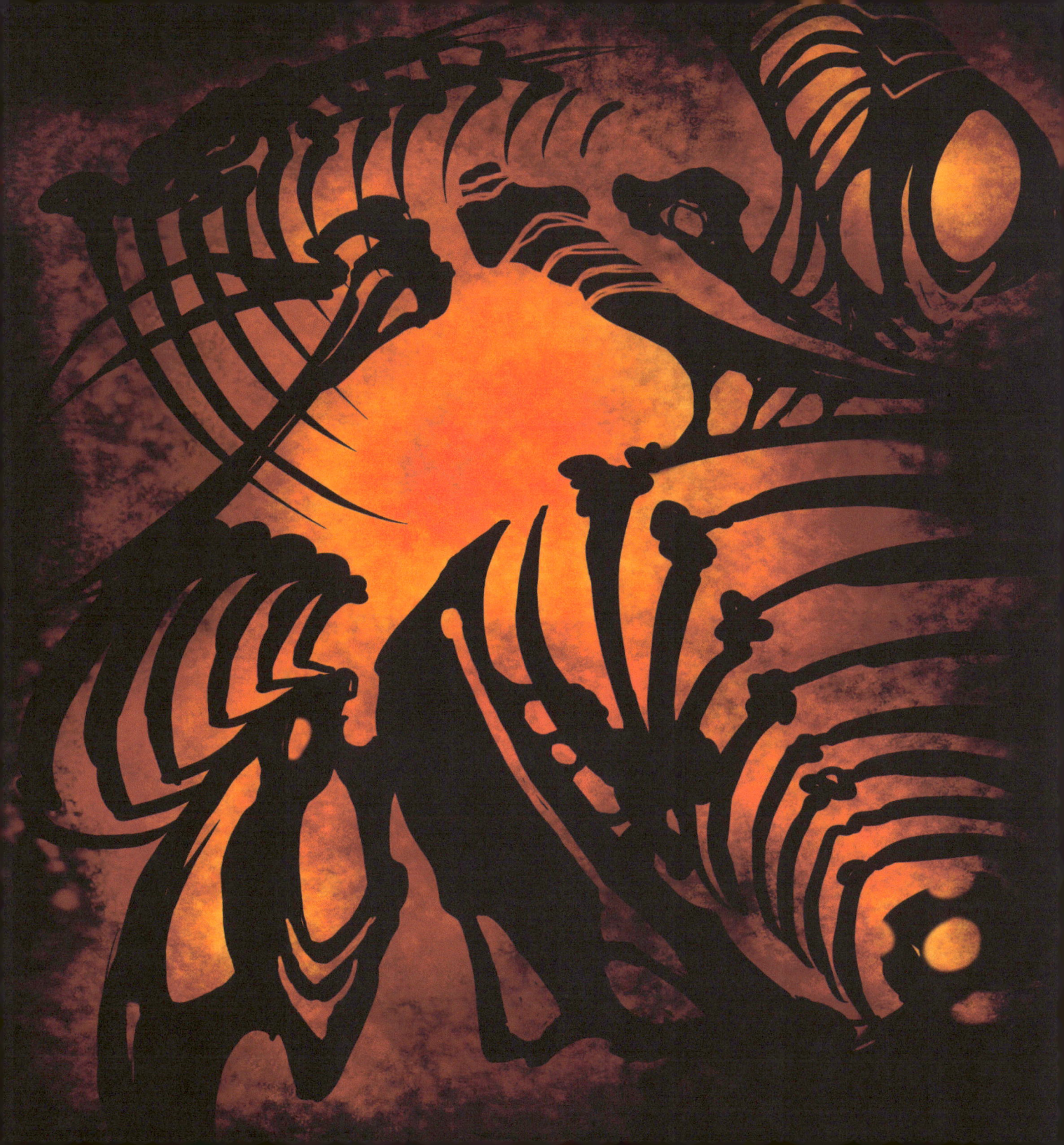

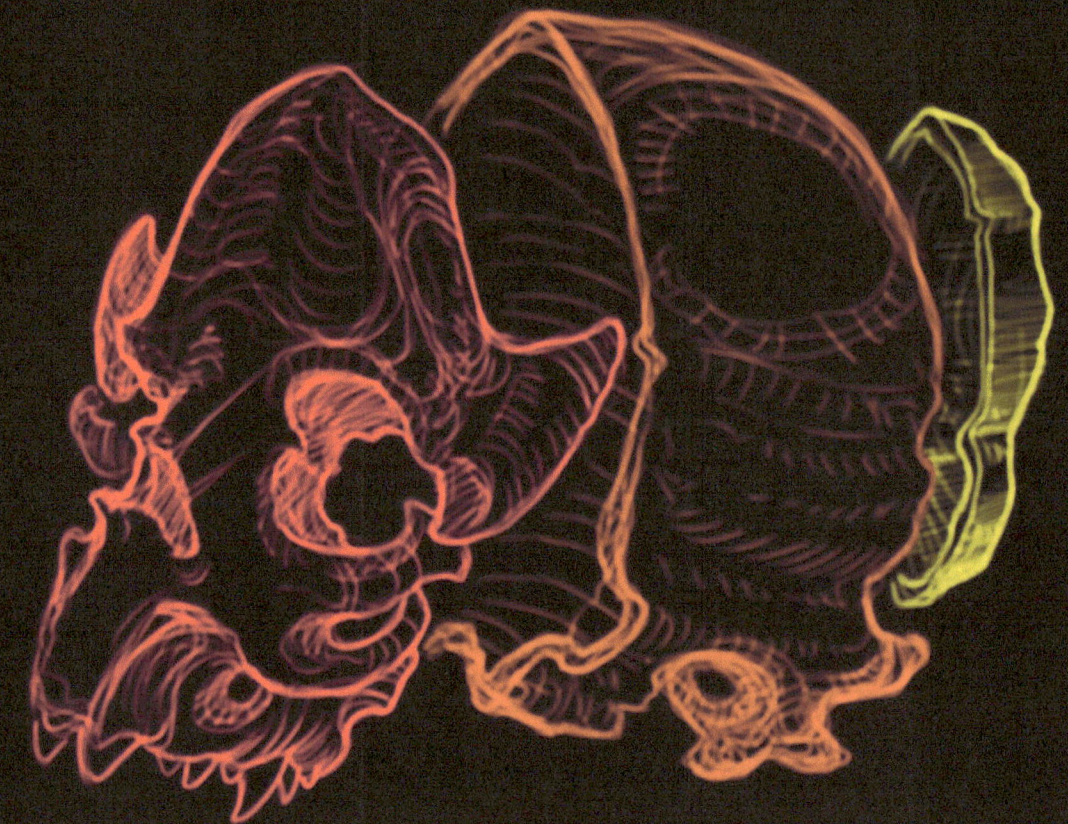

Kevin Harden

www.ingramcontent.com/pod-product-compliance
Lightning Source LLC
Chambersburg PA
CBHW040414220526
45473CB00004B/1235